The Genet Mission

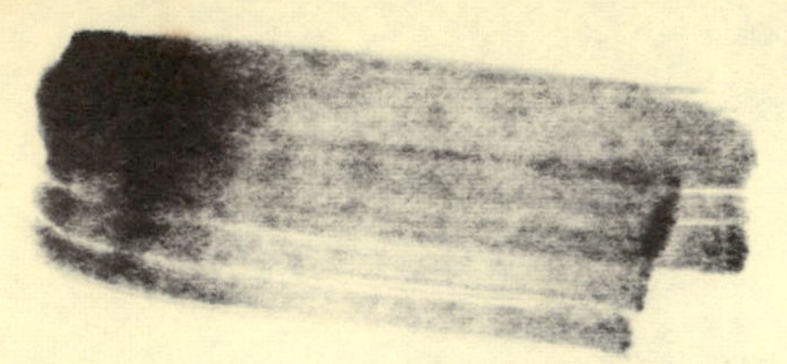

THE NORTON ESSAYS IN AMERICAN HISTORY

Under the general editorship of

HAROLD M. HYMAN

William P. Hobby Professor of American History
Rice University

EISENHOWER AND BERLIN, 1945: THE DECISION TO HALT AT THE ELBE — *Stephen E. Ambrose*

THE MONEY QUESTION DURING RECONSTRUCTION — *Walter T. K. Nugent*

ANDREW JACKSON AND THE BANK WAR — *Robert V. Remini*

THE GREAT BULL MARKET: WALL STREET IN THE 1920's — *Robert Sobel*

THE JACKSONIAN ECONOMY — *Peter Temin*

A NEW ENGLAND TOWN: THE FIRST HUNDRED YEARS — *Kenneth A. Lockridge*

DIPLOMACY FOR VICTORY: FDR AND UNCONDITIONAL SURRENDER — *Raymond G. O'Connor*

THE ORIGINS OF AMERICAN INTERVENTION IN THE FIRST WORLD WAR — *Ross Gregory*

THE IMPEACHMENT AND TRIAL OF ANDREW JOHNSON — *Michael Les Benedict*

THE GENET MISSION — *Harry Ammon*

THE POLITICS OF NORMALCY: GOVERNMENTAL THEORY AND PRACTICE IN THE HARDING–COOLIDGE ERA — *Robert Murray*

The Genet Mission

Harry Ammon

New York W · W · NORTON & COMPANY · INC ·

FIRST EDITION

Published simultaneously in Canada by George J. McLeod Limited, Toronto. Printed in the United States of America.

Library of Congress Cataloging in Publication Data
Ammon, Harry.
The Genet Mission.
Bibliography: p.
1. United States—Foreign relations—1789–1797.
2. Genet, Edmond Charles, 1763–1834. 3. United States —Foreign relations—France. 4. France—Foreign relations—United States. I. Title.
E313.A45 1973 327.44'073 77–95526
ISBN 0–393–05475–6
ISBN 0–393–09420–0 (pbk)

1 2 3 4 5 6 7 8 9 0

Contents

Preface

ON THE MORNING OF APRIL 8, 1793, the wharves and battery of Charleston harbor were the scene of unusual activity as citizens gathered to welcome Edmond Charles Genet, the first Minister to be sent to the United States from the newly formed French Republic.[1] Citizen Genet (the form of address approved in revolutionary France to indicate the equality of all men) had arrived on a forty-four-gun warship, the *Embuscade,* which had anchored outside the harbor. When he stepped ashore, he was cheered by a large and obviously enthusiastic crowd. This was the first of many demonstrations attending his month-long overland journey to Philadelphia. It was a spontaneous outpouring of genuine sympathy for the French Revolution, for Americans sincerely wished that the French people might attain the same happy outcome in their quest for freedom which the Americans had won a decade earlier with France's aid. The fact that Great Britain, America's former oppressor, was numbered among the enemies of France served as a potent stimulant to popular emotion. Charlestonians, in

1. In many standard histories of the United States, Genet's name is frequently spelled with a circumflex accent on the second "e," i.e., Genêt. This usage is incorrect. Genet never used the accent and it does not appear in contemporary records. It made its appearance about 1900. While the original source of the error cannot be pinpointed, it undoubtedly gained currency from the fact that this spelling was used in two widely consulted works: John Spencer Bassett's *Federalist System, 1789–1801* (New York, 1906), Vol. 2 in the American Nation series, and Edward Channing's *History of the United States,* Vol. 4 (New York, 1917). It should be noted that Frederick Jackson Turner, who edited much of Genet's correspondence at the end of the nineteenth century, did not use the circumflex accent.

particular, had bitter memories of the British occupation during the Revolution, when many leading citizens had been deported to the West Indies. Here, too, the descendants of the Huguenots, with their recollections of persecution under the sovereigns of France, were only too happy to render homage to the representative of a republic which had destroyed the privileges of the Roman Catholic Church.[2]

The public reception in Charleston and in other cities as he travelled northward left an indelible impression on Genet. If he ever doubted, and there is no evidence that he did so, the willingness of the United States to render France every form of assistance short of entering the war, he now had what seemed incontestible evidence of American devotion to the cause of France. That this public fervor did not indicate an absolute commitment he had no means of judging. Unfamiliar with both the American people and their government, he tended to assess what he saw in terms valid in the France of his day, where government was totally subject to popular will.[3] Hence his rage, bitterness, and defiance when he discovered that the Washing-

2. See note 1, Chapter 5, below.

3. In a study concerned with diplomacy and American politics, it has not been possible to discuss phases of the French Revolution apart from those directly relevant to Genet's mission. Since references to other aspects of this complex event are unavoidable, it might be useful to summarize the principal phases of the Revolution. The first three stages are usually characterized by the name of the controlling legislative body. The Constituent Assembly (the name adopted by the Estates General after the delegates merged into one house) functioned from June 17, 1789, to October 1, 1791. The Constituent Assembly drafted a constitution creating a constitutional monarchy (October, 1791–August, 1792). During this period the legislative body was known as the Legislative Assembly, which gave way to the National Convention after the destruction of the monarchy in August, 1792. Technically called to draft a republican constitution, the National Convention governed France until 1795. The Convention was at first (until late spring of 1793) controlled by the Girondins and then (until July, 1794) by the Jacobins. Under the Jacobins supreme power was vested in the nine-member Committee of Public Safety dominated by Maximilien Robespierre. He was overthrown in July, 1794, by a conservative coalition anxious to end the Reign of Terror and check the growing radicalism of the Jacobins. The National Convention then drafted a new constitution, which set up a republican government with a five-man executive known as the Directory. The Directory endured until Napoleon seized power in 1799.

ton administration did not demonstrate the same eagerness to rally around France which he thought he had observed among the people.

The Genet mission, which began so happily in Charleston and ended in such anger a few months later, remains one of the most fascinating episodes in the diplomatic history of the United States. Although the conflict between Citizen Genet and President George Washington constitutes the central subject of this book, the story of his mission is something more than the account of the diplomatic contretemps of a blundering agent. The Minister's confrontation with the Washington administration had a profound and lasting impact not only upon foreign policy but also upon domestic politics. The public controversy aroused by Genet's conduct and the demands of his government constituted a vital step in the evolution of the first political parties in the United States. In this context the particular significance of the Genet mission lies in the sharpening of the ideological lines between the two amorphous factions which had emerged in the wake of the dispute over Alexander Hamilton's fiscal program. The debate over Genet, which involved the people as a whole to an unprecedented degree, led to the infusion of a more democratic strain into political processes long dominated by an elite leadership.

The Genet mission had equally important consequences for American foreign policy in both long- and short-range terms. Within the space of a few months after his arrival the French Minister managed to bring the relations between the United States and France to the verge of a rupture. This near disaster cannot be blamed solely on Genet's considerable shortcomings as a diplomat, but can be attributed in large measure to the irreconcilable difference in basic attitudes between two allied states. France and the United States supposedly subscribed to a common set of political principles. Both were dedicated to the maintenance of the then radical principle of republican government based upon popular sovereignty. Yet neither understood that each placed very different interpretations upon the implications of this doctrine. Americans were largely unaware that French revolutionary leaders were espousing a more advanced interpretation of eighteenth-century political liberalism than had ever existed in the United States. French leaders failed to grasp that the American commitment to popular sovereignty and to the doctrine of the rights of man was of a very different order from that current in France. Consequently the outcome of Genet's mission was shaped as much by the nature of the expectations and attitudes of his government as by his personal vagaries. Had he been the very model of diplomatic propriety, it is unlikely that he could have obtained anything more than he did from the Washington administration. Certainly his successors, employing less aggressive means, failed to alter the stance of the American government.

Another equally significant aspect of the Genet mission was its influence on the formulation of long-range policies concerning neutrality. These policies, which endured well into the twentieth century, were forged by President Washington and his cabinet in the midst of domestic controversy and international crisis. It is remarkable that a line of policy framed under so much pressure and in an atmosphere of confusion should have endured so long. The stages in which the American principles of neutrality were formulated provide a rare insight into the process of decision making at the highest political level.

This study of the Genet mission, then, ranges widely, encompassing the broad base of French foreign policy, the condition of American politics before and after the Minister's arrival, the mission itself, and the policies created under pressure in the midst of a bitter national debate. While this study is essentially concerned with international relations and domestic politics, some attention must be given to the agent himself. Genet is commonly depicted as a foolish and impulsive diplomat, whose maladroit behavior compelled Washington to request his recall. This estimate is not unjust, but it is something less than the full truth. Therefore, as a prologue, the reader will find a biographical sketch adding a small but necessary dimension to the understanding of the Genet mission.

HARRY AMMON

Carbondale, Illinois

The Genet Mission

ABBREVIATIONS

In the interest of saving space, the following abbreviations have been used in the footnotes:

AECPEU	Archives Étrangères, Correspondence Politique, États-Unis
ASPFR	*American State Papers, Foreign Relations*
CFM	Correspondence of the French Ministers to the United States, edited by Frederick Jackson Turner
Ford, *Jefferson*	*Writings of Thomas Jefferson,* edited by W. C. Ford
LC	Library of Congress

1

Prologue: In the Shadow of Versailles

EDMOND CHARLES GENET, like most leaders of the republican phase of the French Revolution, came from a comfortable middle-class background.[1] His father, Edmé Jacques Genet, a gifted linguist, was a royal civil servant, who began his career as Secretary Interpreter to the Ministries of War, Marine and Foreign Affairs, a post involving the translation and compilation of reports from foreign sources. A specialist in English affairs, Edmé Jacques attracted attention during the Seven Years' War by his success in collecting accurate data on English naval strength. In 1762, the Minister of Foreign Affairs, the Duc de Choiseul, named him chief of the newly created Bureau of Interpretation in the Ministry of Foreign Affairs.

During the next decade Edmé Jacques concentrated on Anglo-American affairs as the French government watched the disturbances in America in the hope that they might be

1. Material on Genet's early career and family is from Meade Minnigerode, *Jefferson Friend of France, 1793: The Career of Edmond Charles Genet . . .* (New York, 1928); Louis Franklin Genet, "Edmond Charles Genet," *Journal of American History,* VI (1912), 345–67, 489–504, 737–56; J. J. Jusserand, "La Jeunesse de Citoyen Genet," *Revue d'histoire diplomatique,* XLIV (1930), 237–68; MS Memoirs and other papers in the Genet Papers, Library of Congress [hereinafter cited as LC]; Maude H. Woodfin, "Citizen Genet and His Mission" (unpublished Ph.D. thesis, University of Chicago, 1928).

exploited to Great Britain's disadvantage. After the outbreak of the American Revolution the Bureau acted as a clearing house for information on American affairs and as a center for propaganda justifying the rebellion and stressing the commercial advantages for France in supporting the American cause. His office and his home (both located in Versailles where the royal government was centered) were frequented by the American representatives in France—Benjamin Franklin, John Adams, John Paul Jones and Ralph Izard all knew and liked this genial and sympathetic royal official. Franklin worked closely with Edmé Jacques, contributing frequently to the Bureau's propaganda organ, the *Affaires de l'Angleterre et l'Amérique*. The many articles written by Edmé Genet under the guise of a London banker reflected his sympathy for republican institutions.[2] Edmé communicated his enthusiasm to his only son, Edmond Charles, who as a young boy met the American patriots who visited his father.

Edmond Charles Genet was born in Versailles on January 8, 1763. He grew up the spoiled and cosseted darling of his family, idolized by his four sisters and his parents. Educated by tutors, Edmond learned to read English, Swedish, Italian, and Latin by the age of twelve.[3] Not only was he a prodigy, but he was also a dutiful son who unquestioningly accepted his father's plan to educate him for the diplomatic service. This was an exalted ambition for the son of a bourgeois civil servant, for the diplomatic corps was then an aristocratic preserve. The Genets dared aim high, for Henriette (the eldest daughter, eleven years Edmond's senior) held an important position at court, having been named first *femme de chambre* to Queen Marie Antoinette. This post combined the duties of social secretary with those of treasurer for the Queen's privy purse. As a result of Henriette's personal association with the Queen, the Genet

2. Gilbert Chinard, "Adventures in a Library," *Newberry Library Bulletin*, 2nd ser., No. 8 (March, 1951), 223–38.

3. Jusserand, *loc. cit.*, XLIV, 248–50; MS Memoirs, Genet Papers, LC; Minnigerode, *Jefferson*, 10–17. To give Edmond a more acceptable social standing the Queen arranged for an appointment as a Lieutenant in the Royal Dragoons.

family enjoyed greater prestige than that of the ordinary civil servant.[4]

In 1776, Edmond, with the aid of his tutor, published a translation from the Swedish of Olof Celsius' *History of Eric XIV of Sweden.* This work of a thirteen-year-old boy attracted much attention, for the proud father distributed copies to men of importance throughout Europe. The praise it received from rulers (including a gold medal from the King of Sweden), aristocrats, and savants was quite enough to turn young Edmond's head. At fourteen he was given a clerkship in his father's office and awarded the honorary (but prestigious) post of translator to the King's brother. The last phase of Edmond's education began in 1780 when his father sent him on the Grand Tour, a project facilitated by the Queen, who arranged temporary assignments at French embassies in Europe.

The tour commenced in Germany with a sojourn of several months in Frankfort for Edmond to improve his German before he moved to Giessen to attend lectures at the University. He was not impressed by what he saw. The Germans, he wrote his father, were a provincial lot, the students behaving like peasants and the professors nothing but tattered pedants. The food was wretched (he did not like sauerkraut), and Edmond was bored by the all-male gatherings devoted to pipe smoking and beer drinking. More to his taste was the company of the ladies who fussed over this attractive Frenchman, who not only played the harpsichord and sang delightfully, but was a mine of information about the court scandals and the latest fashions to be seen at Versailles. He then moved to Berlin and Vienna. Every-

4. Henriette Genet (better known by her married name of Campan) had a remarkable career. She was particularly close to Marie Antoinette and her memoirs constitute an important source for the reign of Louis XVI. Mme. Campan was genuinely devoted to the Queen, remaining with her royal mistress until Marie Antoinette's imprisonment. Henriette managed to escape arrest during the Reign of Terror, and after the overthrow of Robespierre in 1794 she established a girls' school just outside Paris. Her academy remained the most prestigious finishing school in France until the downfall of Napoleon. See F. Funck-Brentano, ed., *Mémoires de Mme. Campan sur la vie privée de Marie Antoinette* (2 vols., Paris, 1928), I, v–xxiv.

where he was received with the consideration due a royal protégé.[5]

His travels ended in September, 1781, when he returned home because of his father's death. Not yet nineteen, Edmond became chief of the Bureau of Interpretation. Plans for a diplomatic career were put aside, for his inheritance was heavily burdened with debts contracted to pay the dowries of his four sisters. Fortunately his salary of 40,000 livres enabled him to pay off these obligations and also to provide for his mother.[6] His rank as a civil servant and the patronage of the Queen made him a man of consequence. Like his father he was active in a variety of learned societies, including the Academy of Sciences of Paris, the Medical Society of Paris, and the British Royal Society of Antiquaries. He corresponded with German societies and translated their reports for the benefit of French organizations. As an amateur scientist he watched with fascination the balloon ascension of Étienne and Joseph Montgolfier at Versailles on September 19, 1783. This dramatic feat (the second such balloon ascension) excited him with visions of a radically new means of transportation if the direction of flight could be controlled. A month later he read to the Paris Academy of Sciences a paper proposing that the fire used to heat the air in the balloon also be used to heat water in two oversized glass jugs (known as eolipyles) in order to produce a jet of steam capable of propelling the balloon. Although the committee to which this paper was referred reported favorably, neither Genet nor the committee had sufficient mathematical knowledge to realize that the steam pressure generated in this manner would be utterly ineffective as a propulsive force.[7]

5. Minnigerode, *Jefferson,* 51–62.

6. Genet Papers, LC; Woodfin, Genet Mission, 31, fn. 13. The sum of 40,000 livres can be equated in money of that day to $10,000 but the purchasing power was four to six times what it would be today. On comparative money values see J. M. Thompson, *The French Revolution* (Oxford, 1964), viii.

7. Certificates of membership are in Genet Papers, LC. See Greville Bathe, *Citizen Genet, Diplomat and Inventor* (Philadelphia, 1946), 14–16.

Work at the Bureau went on much as it had in his father's time, but with primary emphasis upon English commerce and American political developments. Genet regularly summarized American news and translated such important documents as state constitutions, pamphlets, and speeches. The routine of Genet's job at the Bureau was interrupted early in 1783 and again in the following year by special missions to England. On the first trip he gathered data on English commerce in connection with the peace negotiations which culminated in the Treaty of Paris of 1783, ending the war between Great Britain and France and establishing American independence. The second trip involved a survey of British industrial developments.[8]

His comfortable life as a royal civil servant terminated abruptly in September, 1787, when, in the wake of the drastic economizing measures recommended by Finance Minister Jacques Necker, the Bureau of Interpretation was liquidated and its employees shifted to other bureaus or retired. With the Queen's aid, Genet found another post as Secretary of the Legation in the St. Petersburg Embassy, where he arrived in January, 1788.[9]

On every count except birth Genet seemed cut out for a successful career in the diplomatic service. To solid experience in the Foreign Office he added remarkable linguistic talents, although in an age when French was the language of sovereigns and diplomats that was not an essential qualification. He had a full measure of social graces—polished manners, charm, wit, an engaging personality, and a ready flow of conversation. To these should be added his minor but by no means negligible skills as a harpsichordist and singer. He was quite attractive, moderately tall (5′8″ according to his passport) with clear blue eyes, an aquiline nose, full chestnut hair, and a ruddy complexion. Enthusiastic, energetic, and seemingly well-informed, he made an excellent impression. The Russian Ambassador,

8. Minnigerode, *Jefferson,* 73–79; Bathe, *Genet,* 16, 28.

9. Frederic Masson, *Le Département des Affaires étrangères pendant la révolution* (Paris, 1877), 42; Montmorin (Minister of Foreign Affairs) to Count de Ségur, November 3, 1787, Genet Papers, LC.

the Count de Ségur, whose aristocratic background was impeccable, greeted his bourgeois Secretary of Legation cordially. The Count took his cue from the Minister of Foreign Affairs, the Count de Montmorin, who had written that the Queen had a particular interest in M. Genet. The Count (aware that the Queen would see his letter) promptly reported to his superior that Genet's "form, his bearing and conversation" justified all the praises which had been heaped on the young man.[10] He had only one reservation (expressed years later in his memoirs). He felt that Genet had a "very ardent mind." [11] What the Count did not report, and very probably did not discern, was that the new Secretary's knowledge was extremely superficial, that he lacked steadiness of application (for Genet a project begun was a task completed), and that his judgment was based on impulse rather than reflection. These deficiencies, later so evident, were the result both of temperament and of a superficial education. What he learned easily, he learned brilliantly, but he never acquired the kind of self-discipline needed to study subjects which at first seemed unattractive. His abilities were adequate for a secondary position in the diplomatic service, but insufficient for a post in which he would be required to make critical decisions.

Genet never cut a large figure at the court of Catherine the Great. Even though he became chargé after the Ambassador went home on leave shortly after the beginning of the Revolution in 1789, there was little for him to do except compile commercial reports (a task he executed religiously), write gossipy letters home, and enjoy the amenities of St. Petersburg society. In August, 1791, after receiving the news of Louis XVI's attempted flight and his subsequent return to Paris as a virtual prisoner, the Empress barred Genet from court. At the same time she ordered her Foreign Minister not to receive any com-

10. Quoted in Minnigerode, *Jefferson,* 85.

11. Comte de Ségur, *Memoirs and Recollections . . .* (3 vols., London, 1827), III, 279.

munications from the chargé, whom she described as a "demagogue enragé." [12]

Isolated in St. Petersburg more than a thousand miles from Paris, Genet spoke the same language employed by the republicans in the National Assembly, in the press, and in private conversation. Like so many contemporaries reared in an atmosphere charged with criticism of the outmoded institutions of the *ancien régime,* he was caught up in an ecstatic vision of the utopia about to dawn for the peoples of the world. His dispatches, as Jules Jusserand (a French twentieth-century diplomat) has commented, breathed the "grandiloquence of a *sans-culotte."* [13] The very phrases current in republican circles in France flowed almost instinctively from Genet's pen. That this should be the case was not so very remarkable. The French Revolution, in contrast to most modern political upheavals, was not the work of a dedicated cadre of radicals, but happened, as it were, almost by accident. Once the occasion was presented, a century of discontent voiced by a multitude of writers and orators erupted with fury. They had no need to devise an appropriate rhetoric—the critics of the Enlightenment had provided an ample heritage. That Genet should have espoused the cause of republicanism is not surprising. As a youth he had been exposed to the liberal circles surrounding his father and accepted as axiomatic the notion that societies free of monarchy and aristocracy were the only social orders in which human freedom could flourish. Moreover, Genet, in spite of the Queen's patronage, must have been subjected to a thousand slights simply because he was a bourgeois in a branch of the royal service dominated by the aristocracy. For Genet, as for many other Frenchmen, the Revolution provided a release for long-suppressed resentment.

12. George Clinton Genet, *Washington, Jefferson, and Citizen Genet* (New York, 1899), 7–10; Minnigerode, *Jefferson,* 105–13; MS Memoirs, Genet Papers, LC; quote is from Woodfin, "Genet Mission," 45.

13. Jusserand, "Jeunesse de Genet," *loc. cit.,* XLIV, 239ff; Minnigerode, *Jefferson,* 102ff.

Feeling very much an advance sentinel of the Revolution, Genet reported at length to the Foreign Minister about the activities of the émigrés who flocked to Catherine's court soliciting her support in restoring Louis XVI to full power. His apprehension that the Empress might join the monarchs of Austria and Prussia, who seemed on the verge of coming to the rescue of Louis XVI, was excessive. It is true that Catherine regarded the Revolution as an abomination, but she did not let her sympathies for the plight of the King of France interfere with her plans for annexing Poland, an object more easily achieved if Prussia and Austria were enmeshed with the affairs of France.

The tone Genet maintained in his dispatches was not calculated to win the approval of his superiors, for until a Girondin ministry was installed in April, 1792, the King's ministers were drawn from the ranks of the anti-republicans. Convinced that the only way to end internal turmoil and restore the King's power was through foreign intervention, the Minister of Foreign Affairs was much more concerned with promoting the King's secret correspondence with the Emperor of Austria than in responding to Genet's frantic warnings about émigré plots. When Charles-François Dumouriez (a staunch republican) became Minister of Foreign Affairs in April, 1792, he was appalled to discover sixty of Genet's dispatches lying unopened in his office. Delighted to have at least one member of the diplomatic corps attached heart and soul to the Revolution, Dumouriez promptly wrote the chargé in St. Petersburg to assure him that in the future his dispatches would be given prompt attention.[14]

Although Genet's position in Russia was far from comfortable (he believed that he was constantly watched by Catherine's agents), he felt it his duty to remain at his post to keep the government informed about émigré activities. He also cherished the fanciful notion that somehow he might be instrumental in preventing the Empress from intervening in behalf of Louis XVI. His tenure ended in July, 1792, when the Empress sum-

14. Montmorin to Genet, January 23, 1792, Dumouriez to Genet, March 29, April 20, 27, 1792, all in Genet Papers, LC.

marily ordered him to depart.[15] She had at last occupied the larger part of Poland—a prize reluctantly shared with Austria and Prussia. Although now willing to denounce publicly the revolutionary government of France, Catherine declined to join Prussia and Austria in the military operations under way after France declared war on Austria in April, 1792. Packing up the embassy files, Genet departed for home in a spirit of high-minded self-righteousness. In his own eyes he had been a valiant apostle of liberty persecuted at the hands of one of the most odious European tyrants.

15. He left Russia about July 24, reached Warsaw by August 11, and arrived in Paris in mid-September, 1792.

2

The Girondins in Power, I: The Making of a Minister

GENET REACHED PARIS in the middle of September, 1792, just as the governmental structure of France was undergoing a radical transformation, for the Legislative Assembly had abolished the monarchy after the popular uprising of August 10. Although the Legislative Assembly had ordered the arrest and suspension of the King, the determination of his fate was left to a new body, the National Convention which was summoned to meet on September 20, only a few days after Genet's return home. The National Convention was given the task of governing France while drafting a republican constitution to replace the constitutional monarchy established in 1791. Before disbanding, the Assembly vested executive power in a Provisional Executive Council—an arrangement perpetuated by the Convention when it met. The Executive Council (nominally under the control of committees in the Convention) governed France until April, 1793, when it was subordinated to the newly created Committee of Public Safety.

The republicans had succeeded in destroying the monarchy, but it was by no means certain that the Convention could accomplish anything, for the country, threatened by foreign invasion and beset by internal disorders, seemed on the verge of collapse. In Paris, at the time of Genet's arrival, a contest for power was in progress between the Provisional Executive Council and the Paris Commune (as the radically oriented city government was called) to control the next stage of the

Revolution. The Commune, spurred by Marat and the extreme republicans, had arrested thousands (mostly aristocrats and priests) who were charged with plotting the destruction of France. Early in September—Genet was not yet in Paris—the Commune permitted self-appointed bands of citizens, inflamed by the impassioned rhetoric of Marat, to enter the prisons and administer summary justice to the traitors. In these September massacres (the first reign of terror of the Revolution) more than a thousand were slaughtered. This bloody frenzy was in many ways the result of the panic overwhelming the nation as Austrian and Prussian armies advanced towards Paris. The French army seemed helpless in the face of the disciplined foreign troops. The patriotic enthusiasm of the thousands who had volunteered during the summer was not sufficient to compensate for the loss of the many officers who had emigrated.

At the bleakest moment defeat was transformed into victory on September 20 (the very day set for the meeting of the National Convention), when Dumouriez, who had left the Foreign Office to return to his first profession, turned the invaders back at Valmy. Assuming the offensive, French troops advanced into Belgium and Germany to liberate the enslaved peoples of Europe, as the Convention proclaimed to the world. With the respite provided by Valmy the republican leaders in the Convention set about creating a durable regime, a task rendered difficult by the need to supply the army, by inflation, by food shortages, and by dissension within France.[1]

The National Convention, unlike previous legislative bodies formed since 1789, contained only a sprinkling of aristocrats and priests. Ninety per cent of its membership was drawn from the professional classes (lawyers predominating), businessmen, and civil servants. During its first six months it was dominated

1. I have based my account of the Girondins largely upon Georges Lefebvre, *The French Revolution from its Origins to 1793* (2 vols., New York, 1962–64). I have also found the following especially useful: Eloise Ellery, *Brissot de Warville: A Study in the History of the French Revolution* (New York, 1915), Vassar Semi-Centennial Series; J. M. Thompson, *French Revolution* (Oxford, 1964); A. Aulard, *The French Revolution: A Political History* (4 vols., London, 1910).

by the Girondins, a loosely affiliated group of deputies who owed their prestige to their republicanism and to a reputation for patriotism earned as the result of their advocacy of war against Austria. The Girondins, familiarized with Genet's political views by Dumouriez, welcomed him as a martyr to the whims of the tyrant of Russia and as the only French diplomat "who had dared act like a free man" (in the words of the Diplomatic Committee of the Convention) by upholding the principles of the Revolution.[2] Genet was drawn to the Girondins, not just because they were in a position to advance his career, but also because he shared their aspirations. In view of his identification with the Girondins, it is essential for an understanding of his conduct as Minister to the United States to take a closer look at the men who governed France from September, 1792, until driven from power by the Jacobins in the following June.

The Girondins can best be described as a band of like-minded men generally agreed about the measures needed to consolidate the Revolution and advance the cause of human freedom. In the 783-member National Convention they numbered only 160, but they constituted the largest cohesive element. They were only slightly more numerous, however, than their greatest rivals, the Jacobins, with whom they battled during the winter of 1792–93 for the control of the uncommitted majority—the so-called Marsh or Plain. Since the sessions of the Convention were ordinarily attended by less than half of the deputies, it was relatively easy for the Girondins to obtain control.

The Girondins owed their name to the accidental circumstance that several of their better known spokesmen lived in or near the city of Bordeaux in the department of the Gironde. Frequently, and with just as much accuracy, they were called *Brissotins, Buzotists,* or *Rolandists* after three of their most prominent leaders. It has often been asserted that the Girondins lacked either a common program or a set of principles

2. Genet to Jefferson, July 4, 1797 (letter not sent), printed in Minnigerode, *Jefferson,* 415–16.

other than a naive faith in the redeeming power of republican institutions, but this generalization falls short of the truth. They were in fact ever ready with new theories and programs, but what they so conspicuously lacked—and this in a curious way constituted one of the strongest bonds uniting them—was the ability to translate their aspirations into practical measures. They tended to talk in large terms, reveling in noble ideals and intoxicating themselves, as Genet did in America, with rhetorical visions of the approaching utopia. As Georges Lefebvre has remarked, there was always an air of flightiness (there could be no more apt description of Genet's behavior in America) about the Girondins which made them incapable of coping with the realities of France's political situation. They were constantly baffled that the reiteration of the platitudes of republicanism failed to solve the complex problems facing the nation.[3]

The Jacobins, inveterate enemies of the Girondins, spoke much the same language and relied upon similar revolutionary slogans, but the Jacobin leaders understood that measures framed in accordance with purest republican theory might have the most disastrous practical consequences. The Jacobins succeeded in rescuing France from invasion and domestic rebellion in 1793 not solely because of a more pragmatic approach but also because they had no scruples about suppressing the political opposition so generously tolerated by the Girondins in the name of liberty. The Girondins possessed a nobility of spirit, a true humanity, an unwavering idealism, which, in spite of all their shortcomings, make them among the most appealing figures of the French Revolution.

The Girondins came into prominence in 1791 through their advocacy of war with Austria. They believed that the war would not only weaken the monarchy but also advance the cause of liberty by arousing the Emperor's subjects to revolt. To the subsequent embarrassment of the Girondins the war cry was taken up by the monarchists, who welcomed foreign intervention, even

3. Lefebvre, *French Revolution,* I, 215.

by the Queen's detested Austrian relatives, as the sole means of restoring Louis XVI's power. Robespierre and the Jacobins opposed the war simply because they felt that the French army, demoralized by the defection of the large numbers of experienced officers who had joined the ranks of the émigrés, could not stand up to disciplined soldiers. Moreover, they contended that war would pave the way for a restoration of the monarchy to its former position.

There were other less apparent but equally fundamental differences between the Jacobins and the Girondins. Although both were drawn from the middle class, the Girondin leadership reflected the temper of the great commercial cities on the periphery of France—Bordeaux, Toulon, Marseille, whose interests lay in foreign trade. These cities were very different from Paris where industry and retail trade prevailed. The Girondins never felt at ease with the industrialists, shopkeers, and urban proletariat of the capital. The Jacobins, however, although by no means all Paris born, won the confidence of the Parisians by seeming (if only from necessity) more responsive to the interests of the common people. Thus the Jacobins, after the uprising of August, 1792, did not share the Girondin fear of a republic dominated by the mob. In terms of general economic policy, the Girondins, as befitted spokesmen of the commercial sector, were uncompromising advocates of free trade, whereas the Jacobins, faithful to the industrial orientation of Paris, approved the continuance of the mercantilist regulatory measures of the Old Regime. The Jacobins and Girondins also disagreed about the proper structural principle upon which to organize the republic. The Girondins, reflecting the provincial distrust of Paris and of centralized authority, wished to preserve the decentralized, federative structure established by the constitution of 1791. The Jacobins, on the other hand, sought to end the limited local self-government and vest absolute power in the national government.

After the dispute over the declaration of war, the Girondins ceased attending the Jacobin club, preferring the more congenial environment of the salons established by Mme.

Dodun for Pierre Vergniaud, a deputy from Bordeaux and the most brilliant Girondin orator in the Convention, or that of the wife of Jean Marie Roland, the Secretary of the Interior in the Executive Council. Both salons were political in character with an exclusively masculine attendance. The salon of Manon Phlipon Roland, an attractive woman of thirty-eight with intellectual tastes, was the more important of the two. She exerted a powerful influence over her husband (some twenty years her senior), drafting many of his state papers. Although Roland, a former royal inspector of manufactures and the author of an esteemed dictionary of manufacturing, seemed a dull and pedantic figure beside his glamorous wife, they shared a deep romantic attachment to the cause of republicanism and were stirred by the same grandiose visions of the coming liberation of mankind. Her personal antipathies—she disliked both Robespierre and Danton—played an important role in widening the chasm between the Girondins and the Jacobins. Because her interference in public affairs was so much resented, she was guillotined after the downfall of the Girondins. Her husband, faithful to the romantic attachment of their common political dreams, committed suicide when he learned of her death.[4]

The star of Mme. Roland's salon was Jacques Pierre Brissot de Warville, whose book on America had awakened her admiration long before she met the author.[5] While it is true that the Girondins did not have an acknowledged leader, no one person more accurately epitomized their program, aspirations, ambitions, and indeed their very weaknesses than Brissot. Born in Chartres (his father was a restaurateur) in 1754, he moved to Paris when he was twenty, adding "de Warville" to his name to suggest aristocratic antecedents. Working as a free-lance journalist, which then meant hiring out one's pen to anyone willing to pay, he met most of the advanced thinkers of the

4. For Mme. Roland see Lefebvre, *French Revolution,* I, *passim;* and Madeleine Jacquemaire, *The Life of Madame Roland* (New York, 1930).

5. On Brissot see Ellery, *Brissot;* and J. M. Thompson, *Leaders of the French Revolution* (New York, 1962).

day. Brissot's closest associate was Étienne Clavière, a Swiss banker exiled from Geneva because of his liberal political views. In 1788 they collaborated on a study of Franco-American commerce in which they recommended a policy of free trade as more advantageous to France than the existing restrictive system. Later they established a Gallo-American Society to propagate their views. Brissot was also deeply committed to the abolition of slavery in the French colonies, founding the *Societé des Amis des Noirs* to foster his proposals. Among the members were some of the most distinguished men of the day —Lafayette, Mirabeau, and Condorcet (later a Girondin). Thomas Jefferson, the American Minister in Paris, declined Brissot's invitation to join. He approved the aims of the society and thought highly of Brissot, but considered membership incompatible with his official position. As a result of the continued pressure exerted by the Society the Legislative Assembly enfranchised the free mulattoes in Santo Domingo.

Brissot shared the enthusiasm of French republicans for the United States, which they cherished as the first nation to replace a tyrannical government with one based upon free institutions. Theirs was an idealized view of America based upon the erroneous conviction that America, in revolting against George III, had been inspired by the same abstract principles of republicanism and the same precepts of natural law which were now stirring the people of France. The unreal view of the United States current in France owed much to the romanticized image presented in St. John Crèvecoeur's *Letters of An American Farmer* which appeared in 1783. Crèvecoeur, who had resided in the middle colonies and moved in Quaker circles, praised the Americans for their equalitarianism, simple republican manners, and freedom from the errors, intolerance, and prejudice of the Old World.[6]

Brissot (one of the few Girondins with a firsthand knowledge of America) spent several months in the United States

6. Durand Echeverria, *Mirage in the West: A History of the French Image of American Society to 1815* (Princeton, 1957), 146–61.

in 1788 purchasing public securities for a syndicate organized by Clavière. In the published account of his travels (largely confined to the middle states) he provided more specific details than Crèvecoeur, but the same idyllic picture emerged. He saw much of the Quakers, and took their equalitarianism and their antislavery views to be somehow the mark of the true American. He attributed the prosperity and freedom which he saw everywhere to the superiority of American political institutions, a conclusion characteristic of the Girondin habit of oversimplification. Although he did not travel in the West, he was aware of Western discontent over Spain's refusal to permit free navigation of the Mississippi. His American experience gave him the reputation of being an expert on American affairs, and when the Girondins attained power in the autumn of 1792, Brissot, as a member of the Diplomatic Committee of the Convention, became the responsible architect of French policy towards the United States.

Brissot returned to France too late to stand for election to the Estates General which met in May, 1789, but he rapidly became a potent force as an organizer of public protests and as the editor of one of the most successful Parisian newspapers, *Le Patriote Français*. In the columns of his paper he gave free reign to his conviction that republican government based upon universal manhood suffrage would prevail. He also continued his assault on slavery and restrictive commercial regulations. Among the more notable contributors to his paper were Thomas Paine, Clavière, Condorcet, the Abbé Grégoire and the Rolands. In 1791, he moved into the forefront of the republican leadership as a member of the Legislative Assembly, the body which governed France until August, 1792, when the constitutional monarchy established by the Constitution of 1791 was overthrown.

Upon his arrival in Paris in mid-September, 1792, Genet entered the Girondin inner circle. Mme. Roland, who made a hero of anyone who talked republicanism, welcomed him into her salon. She urged his merits on all her friends, praising his "solid" and "enlightened mind" and the "sweetness, justice, grace, and reason" of his conversation, all the more pleasing because it was without "affectation or pedantry." [7] Brissot, familiar with the chargé's dispatches from Russia, was equally enchanted with the "democrat Genet." [8] In response to a request from the Girondins, Genet drafted a report for the Ministry of Foreign Affairs on the reorganization of the diplomatic service. He proposed that the title of "Ambassador" be eliminated, leaving as the highest rank that of "Minister"—a suggestion possibly inspired by the usage of the United States. He also recommended that all promotions to Minister be made from the rank of Secretary of the Legation, in short, the diplomatic service should be governed by rules similar to those controlling advancement in the civil service.[9]

The fact that his sisters (then hiding in the country to avoid arrest) had been so closely associated with the royal family did not hinder his advancement. There were few indeed without questionable political or social connections. Genet's flamboyant professions of republican faith were a sufficient passport in an age when words counted as much as deeds. If a further proof of his patrotism was needed, he provided it by selling the gold medal sent him by the King of Sweden and using the funds to outfit volunteers for the front.[10] His advancement was immediate. On October 10 he was named Minister to the Hague, but the position never materialized because of the likelihood that the French troops then invading Belgium would advance into Holland. Late in October he was in Switzerland on a special mission (he had the rank of adjutant general) to the commander of the French army. It was shortly

7. Quoted in William Frederick Keller, "American Politics and the Genet Mission, 1793–1794" (unpublished Ph.D. thesis, University of Pittsburgh, 1951), 83.

8. So Brissot referred to him in the Legislative Assembly in May, 1792. Woodfin, "Genet Mission," 60.

9. Copy of the report dated October 21, 1792, is in Genet Papers, LC.

10. Extract from the register of the municipality of Versailles, September 26, 1792, *ibid.*

after his return early in November that he was appointed Minister to the United States.[11]

His selection was an indication of the confidence which French leaders had in his ability, patriotism, and love of liberty, as the Diplomatic Committee proclaimed in his instructions. The American mission was regarded as an important one involving both an emotional attachment and practical objectives. In view of the admiration on the part of Brissot and the Girondins for France's ally, it is not surprising that an attempt should be made to draw the two republics into a closer understanding. What real profit was there for France in seeking close relations with European monarchs who feared and condemned the Revolution? Brissot considered it axiomatic that republics, like individuals dedicated to the cause of freedom, shared an identity of interest and the most intimate fraternal ties.

Girondin American policy was formulated at a moment when French leaders were entranced by an ecstatic vision of the approaching worldwide revolution which would establish republican governments for all nations. They envisaged a universal republic not in the sense that all men would be united under one government, but a kind of mystical union created by the acceptance of universally valid political principles. It was under the aegis of this religion of humanity that the Legislative Assembly, just before its term expired in August, had conferred French citizenship upon a dozen individuals distinguished for their antimonarchical and republican activities. Among those honored were the Englishmen William Priestly, Jeremy Bent-

11. Dumouriez had previously appointed Bonnecarrère, a Foreign Office functionary, but the Girondins, who did not like him, canceled his appointment as soon as they came to power in August. Their disapproval seems to have been both personal and political. According to Gouverneur Morris he was a man of bad character "stain'd by infamous vices." Mme. Roland considered him a gambler and a roué quite unsuited for the American post. He also seems to have been on friendly terms with the Jacobins. Gouverneur Morris to Jefferson, August 16, 1792, in Gouverneur Morris, *Diary of the French Revolution,* Beatrix Cary Davenport, ed. (2 vols., Boston, 1939), II, 494; Frederick A. Schminke, *Genet: The Origins of His Mission in America* (Toulouse, France, 1929), 62–63; Masson, *Département des affaires étrangères,* 150–58.

ham, and Thomas Paine, and a trio of Americans—Washington, Madison, and Alexander Hamilton. A few weeks later Joel Barlow, an American who had gone to France to sell lands for the Scioto Company and was now an ardent convert to the Girondin world view, was added to the list.

In accomplishing the goal of universal liberty, the Girondins envisaged France's role as something more than merely setting a moral example. Although they did not propose to conduct an all out war on the monarchs of the world, they were willing to stimulate revolts and assist peoples ready to fight for freedom. This was the justification for the decision to permit French troops to advance into Germany and Belgium after Valmy: a war of liberation, not of conquest. On November 19, the very day on which the Convention confirmed Genet as Minister to the United States, a decree was approved promising brotherly assistance to people seeking freedom. "We cannot rest," Brissot declared, "until all Europe is ablaze. What puny projects were those of Richelieu . . . compared with the worldwide risings, the gigantic revolutions, that we are called upon to achieve." [12] In this context it was perfectly logical for the Girondins to expect that the Americans would eagerly assist in the liberation of the oppressed peoples in the Spanish and British colonies.

12. Thompson, *French Revolution,* 336.

3

The Girondins in Power, II: The Girondin American Policy

IN WORKING OUT A NEW American policy, Brissot and the Girondins assumed that France's ally and sister republic would willingly offer fraternal assistance in the war against tyrants. While the notion of fraternal assistance was rather vague and without precedents to guide its implementation, it clearly did not involve the participation of the United States in the war. In the first place, as much as the Girondins were intrigued by grandiose visions of an alliance of free peoples against the despots of the world, they were not so infatuated as to forget that the United States was too weak to render effective military aid. Secondly, the commercially oriented Girondins rightly understood that the most effective contribution of the United States would be as a neutral carrying foodstuffs desperately needed in France.

The Girondins did expect the American government to assist France through advance payment of the debt incurred during the American Revolution. The Washington administration had already made advances to the French Minister, Jean Baptiste de Ternant, to enable him to aid refugees fleeing from the slave rebellion in Santo Domingo. He also received funds for supplies for the French forces in the island colony. Now that France was a republic, it seemed logical to anticipate still larger advances. With this in mind Foreign Minister Le-Brun and Minister of Finances Clavière called on Gouverneur Morris (the American Minister in Paris) late in August, 1792. Morris, whose sympathies were openly with the monarchy, regarded the Girondins as a "set of damned rascals." Consequently, he summarily refused their request, alleging that he lacked authority to make such an agreement. Particularly offensive to the Girondins was his comment that he doubted his authority to deal with the Provisional Executive Council since he had been accredited to Louis XVI. Angered by Morris's oblique questioning of the legitimacy of the new regime, Le-Brun replied so sharply that Morris threatened to depart for home at once. Much as the Girondins disliked the American Minister, they preferred to avoid a rupture which might delay the new era in Franco-American relations planned for Genet's mission. LeBrun sent Morris a second letter, which, if not precisely an apology, sufficiently mollified the American Minister so that he remained in Paris. The Girondins, who did not expect to accomplish anything through him, kept Morris at a distance. It was expected, of course, that Genet would not encounter any obstacles in America to the French request for advance payments on the debt.[1]

Genet's instructions, which summed up Girondin policy towards the United States, were drafted by Brissot and his colleagues on the Diplomatic Committee after a thorough review of the files in the Ministry of Foreign Affairs. The Committee was assisted by the Minister of Foreign Affairs, Pierre LeBrun, whom Dumouriez had placed in charge of the Foreign Office section dealing with the United States. Genet also participated, advising the committee and using the opportunity to take extensive notes on the correspondence of his predecessors

1. Morris, *Diary*, II, 528–46, August 19–September 6, 1792; Alexander DeConde, *Entangling Alliance, Politics and Diplomacy under George Washington* (Durham, N. C., 1958), 320–24. Morris referred the matter to Washington, who authorized an advance of $318,000 to Ternant in March. See Dumas Malone, *Thomas Jefferson and His Time* (4 vols., New York, 1948–), III, 51–53.

in America. The only other person who seems to have been consulted was Thomas Paine, who arrived in Paris in September to take the seat to which he had been elected in the National Convention.[2]

As a result of their research in the diplomatic files the Girondins learned that relations between the two nations had steadily deteriorated since the end of the American Revolution. Not only had there been some mutual disappointments, but the Americans had taken offense at the behavior of several diplomats resident in the United States. One, the Count de Moustier, had so outraged members of Congress by his hauteur and by his supposed immorality (it was believed that his sister-in-law was his mistress) that his recall had been requested in 1788. In the decade after the American Revolution, Americans had been disappointed by France's unwillingness to grant additional commercial favors and by the failure of the King's representatives to do anything but express vague wishes for the future well-being of the United States. France, too, was exasperated with her ally and resented the fact that French ships were charged the same tonnage duties as the vessels of nations which did not have commercial treaties with the United States. France's protest that this was contrary to the commercial treaty of 1778 did not bring amelioration.

It was recognized on both sides of the Atlantic that the best remedy would be a new treaty, yet neither government made very meaningful gestures in that direction. The National Assembly resolved in 1791 that the King should negotiate new commercial agreements with the United States, but the industrialists and supporters of the old restrictive system still had enough influence to prevent immediate implementation of the legislative resolve. Consequently, Moustier's replacement, Count Jean Baptiste Ternant, was not empowered to discuss commercial issues. If the subject was raised, he was instructed to request the transfer of negotiations to Paris, a suggestion not at all to the liking of Secretary of State Thomas Jefferson,

2. Ellery, *Brissot,* 314–16.

who did not feel that the matter should be entrusted to Gouverneur Morris. Ternant, who realized that commercial issues must be resolved before relations between the two nations could be improved, broached the subject on his own authority. When he approached Jefferson early in 1792, he found the Secretary of State, once an advocate of an extended commercial agreement, unwilling to outline provisions acceptable to the United States. Jefferson saw no point in stating American terms to an agent who did not have the power to negotiate—to do so would destroy the bargaining position of the United States. The fact that Hamilton, to whom Ternant had spoken, strongly favored such a statement made Jefferson doubly reluctant. He suspected (quite correctly) that Hamilton wished to use a hypothetical negotiation with France as an excuse for seeking a commercial treaty with Great Britain. At Washington's insistence, Jefferson outlined to Ternant a plan which would in effect grant the citizens of each nation almost the same privileges as natives.[3]

Ternant's dispatches, particularly his account of the interview with Jefferson, convinced the Girondins that the ideal way for a rapprochment with the United States would be to accede to the American wish for a new treaty. What better way to inaugurate the new era of Franco-American understanding than with a treaty placing the merchants of each nation on a footing of equality. Such a plan had the virtue of serving the best interests of France while at the same time providing a suitable expression of the Girondin conviction that the principles of free trade were those most harmonious with republican theory.

While reviewing the Foreign Office files, the members of the Diplomatic Committee turned up records revealing Louis XVI's attempt to make a secret agreement with England on the eve of the peace negotiations ending the American Revolution.

3. DeConde, *Entangling Alliance,* 140–68; George F. Zook, "Proposals for a New Commercial Treaty between France and the United States," *South Atlantic Quarterly,* VIII (1909), 267–83; Malone, *Jefferson,* III, 397–98.

The discovery that France had urged the British government to cede the region west of the Alleghenies to Spain rather than to the United States, delighted rather than shocked the Girondins, for it was the kind of perfidy to be expected of a monarchy. They now planned to expose this plot so that Americans would realize that Louis XVI had sustained the United States during its Revolution out of self-interest, and that once the war was over the King's only objective had been to inhibit the expansion of republicanism.

The instructions prepared for Genet, which were completed by mid-December, were in two parts.[4] The first section, so flamboyantly rhetorical that one historian has ascribed it to Genet, although it could as well be the work of any Girondin gifted with a free verbal flow, was intended for publication so that Americans (and the world) would be impressed by the noble objectives of his mission.[5] The second portion, a confidential supplement couched in more restrained language, touched specifically upon the details of his mission and made practical suggestions about the Minister's line of conduct. The instructions began with a minor error, which reflected the Girondin vagueness about American institutions. Genet's letter of accreditation was addressed to Congress and not to the President, on the mistaken assumption that Congress, like the National Convention, was the repository of the sovereign will of the people and hence possessed all power. It was inconceivable to the Girondins that the American executive enjoyed an independent area of authority in foreign affairs, for this was

4. Printed in "Correspondence of the French Ministers to the United States, 1797–1797," Frederick J. Turner, ed., *Annual Report of the American Historical Association for the Year 1903,* II (Washington, D. C., 1904), II, 202–11. [Hereinafter cited as *CFM*]. They are unsigned and undated and are technically the work of the Diplomatic Committee as approved by the Executive Council. The first section was probably completed by December 22, the day on which the National Convention adopted an address to President Washington which touches on subjects in the instructions. Details concerning the purchase of grain, etc., were covered in special instructions drafted by the ministries involved.

5. Keller, "Genet Mission," 94–97, makes this suggestion.

an arrangement smacking of monarchical institutions. It was a point which Genet never properly understood even after six months in the United States.

Genet's instructions defined the broad objective of his mission as the strengthening of the bonds which had long united the two nations, although they had been neglected as a result of the duplicity and Machiavellianism of the King, who had sought to check the growth of free institutions in America. As proof the authors of the instructions divulged the news that Louis XVI had conspired with the British to prevent the Americans from obtaining Canada and the Trans-Allegheny West. Now that republicans had supplanted the "vile despots," Genet was authorized to announce frankly and openly that the people of France were "rejecting everything associated with the diplomacy of the past. . . ." and thus opening the way for a new era in the relations of the two republics. How was this to be done? First, Genet was to propose "a national pact in which the two peoples would amalgamate their commercial and political interests and establish an intimate concert, which would promote the extension of the Empire of liberty, guarantee the sovereignty of all peoples, and punish the powers still retaining colonial systems by refusing to admit their ships to the harbors of the two contracting nations." The exact nature of the political commitment was unspecified, but presumably the Girondins expected it to be in the form of a joint declaration affirming the responsibility of all republican peoples to encourage the liberation of mankind. Such an alliance, "energetically supported by the people of France," would not only pave the way for the "liberation of Spanish America" but also "open the Mississippi to the inhabitants of Kentucky, deliver our brothers in Louisiana from the tyrannical yoke of Spain, and perhaps add the glorious star of Canada to the American constellation." Republican virtue was not to be without practical rewards. If these temptations were insufficient to induce the Americans to conclude a treaty, then Genet was to remind them that the fate of liberty in the New World was dependent upon the victory of France in the Old World. Was it not probable that Great Britain, if she succeeded in destroying republicanism in France, would make the United States the next object of her concern?

If Congress still hesitated, then Genet was to initiate "all measures which comported with his position" to "germinate" the spirit of liberty and independence in Louisiana, Florida, and Canada. It was assumed that the Kentuckians, so long excluded from the navigation of the Mississippi, would eagerly organize expeditions for the liberation of Louisiana. He was also directed to obtain advance payments on the American debt to purchase grain and other supplies for Santo Domingo and for France. As a final note, Genet was told to avoid the "ridiculous disputes" over rank and etiquette characteristic of the diplomats of the Old Regime, yet he was not to lose sight of the prerogatives and honor due France.

The second section of his instructions, restrained and pragmatic in character, seems to have been drafted by someone familiar with recent developments in the United States—possibly Louis G. Otto, formerly chargé in Philadelphia and presently awaiting an appointment in the Foreign Office.[6] In the supplement Genet was warned that the uncertainty of the international situation and the influence of the pro-British party on the administration would probably lead to a delay in the negotiation of the fraternal agreement proposed by the Girondins. If this proved the case, he was instructed to insist upon a rigid enforcement of articles 17, 21 and 22 of the Treaty of Commerce and Amity of 1778. These were the sections in which each nation agreed to permit the privateers and prizes of the other free entry while excluding those of the enemies of the two powers. In view of the importance of Anglo-American trade and the large number of English vessels in American ports, he was reminded of the importance of impressing on the consuls the need for viligance in detecting infractions of the treaty of 1778.

Genet was also cautioned to be circumspect in his dealings with pro-French public officials. It was essential that he "scrupulously observe the forms established for official communi-

6. On Otto see Masson, *Département des affaires étrangères,* 242–43.

cations between the government and foreign agents and never engage in any move or proposals which might offend free Americans concerning their constitution which differs in many respects from the principles established in France." This was sensible advice, but Genet does not seem to have regarded it as applicable to the objectives outlined in his instructions, which were in many ways at odds with this warning. Consequently, when the Washington administration differed with France's interpretation of the treaty of 1778, Genet deemed it his duty to attempt to bypass presidential directives, even to the length of a direct appeal to the people. The supplementary instructions concluded by authorizing him to issue commissions for officers participating in the expedition against Louisiana and also to commission privateers in American ports.

To underscore the generous intent of French policy, on December 22 the Convention approved an address to the President expressing the pleasure Frenchmen experienced in enlarging France's understanding with a republic founded on the same principles. Emphasis was given to the new diplomacy by exposing Louis XVI's duplicity towards the United States. Reassuringly, the address declared that France did not expect the United States to participate in the European war—a point not explicitly stated in Genet's instructions. Therefore, those provisions of the Treaty of Alliance of 1778 binding the two nations to a mutual guarantee of each other's possession in the event either was involved in war of a defensive character were not to be invoked. As a more substantial token of France's sincerity, the Convention in mid-February lifted all restrictions on American goods and ships in French ports.

Before Genet left for America late in February, LeBrun and Otto (now in the Foreign Office) wrote several letters amplifying his instructions. Le Brun suggested that Genet counteract the influence of the pro-English element by inserting anonymous pieces in the press in cities where the pro-French element was weak. The new diplomacy, on this point at least, was not a departure from that of the past, for Louis XVI's representatives had frequently sought to control American opinion. Somewhat at variance with the original line of his instructions was the recommendation that he place complete confidence in Jefferson, Washington, and Madison, all known to be sympathetic to the French Revolution. LeBrun also touched on a subject not previously discussed—the recall of Gouverneur Morris. The Foreign Minister did not make his removal mandatory, suggesting that Genet take up the matter on a suitable occasion and not in a way which might give offense.[7]

Genet's instructions were completed by the end of December and a frigate, *L'Embuscade,* readied for his voyage at Rochefort, but nearly a month elapsed before he left Paris. The delay was deliberately arranged by the Girondins who hoped the Minister might take Louis XVI and his family into exile in the United States. Genet was a party to this plan, which was typical of the Girondin habit of reducing politics to romantic fantasy. When the king was brought to trial on the charge of treason before the National Convention in December, it was soon apparent that the central issue was not the question of his guilt or innocence, but what the punishment should be. Having destroyed the monarchy, the Girondins wished to spare the King, for their quarrel had been with the institution and not the incumbent. The inclination toward mercy was not prompted either by a dislike of violence or a sentimental attachment to the family Capet, but by the realization that sending the King to the guillotine would intensify hostility abroad and increase domestic opposition to the republic. The proposal that the King be sent to America was apparently broached to Genet by Dumouriez, who had left his command to lobby in Paris against the death sentence. The plan also had the active support of Thomas Paine, the most vigorous advocate of clemency in the Convention. How far Brissot and other Girondins were implicated is difficult to say. In the face of the Jacobin cry that advocates of leniency were enemies of liberty, the Girondins wavered. Rather than risk loss of power, most (including

7. Letters dated February 3, 24, 1793, Archives des Affaires Étrangères, Correspondance Politique, États-Unis. [Hereinafter cited as AECPEU.] See also Minnigerode, *Jefferson,* 148–54.

Vergniaud and Brissot) voted for the death penalty on January 18, 1793. After the failure of Paine's last minute effort to obtain a reprieve, the King was guillotined on January 21. That very night Genet left the city, arriving at Rochefort two days later. In the tense and fear-ridden atmosphere created by the King's trial, it is not surprising that the guards at the city gates stopped the Minister and searched his luggage before allowing him to continue his journey.[8]

During his month long wait in Paris, Genet busied himself with a multitude of private and public concerns. He drafted an elaborate plan for the reorganization of the consular service and spent many hours studying the files of the Ministry of Foreign Affairs. He renewed his wardrobe, ordered furniture, table linen, wines, dishes, and arranged for two carriages to be sent to Rochefort. He also packed his family papers and a vast quantity of documents from the files of the legation in St. Petersburg—all of which he took to America. One of his major concerns was to arrange for a portion of his salary of 60,000 livres to be paid his mother, whom he settled in the country. The balance was turned over to a business agent to invest in confiscated émigré property.[9]

The postponement of Genet's departure provided Paine with an opportunity to present him to Gouverneur Morris. Although Morris was irked by LeBrun's failure to notify him officially of Genet's appointment, he was sufficiently curious to invite the new Minister to dinner. Prior to this Morris had reported to the President that the new Minister was but a parvenu, a former clerk, who owed his previous advancement to royal patronage and now obtained the appointment in America as *"the best harbor during the storms."*[10] After meeting Genet, his reaction was not much different. While Morris's comment

8. Morris, *Diary,* II, 594; Schminke, *Genet Mission,* 97–98; Minnigerode, *Jefferson,* 133–35; Ellery, *Brissot,* 322–24; L. Didier, "Le Citoyen Genet," *Revue des Questions Historiques, XCII* (1912), 69–70; MS Memoirs, Genet Papers, LC.

9. Genet Papers, LC. He also received 30,000 livres for his outfit. He was required to provide housing for the secretaries of legation.

10. Morris to Washington, December 28, 1792, Morris, *Diary,* II, 594.

that Genet had the "manners and looks of an upstart" reflected his dislike of French republicans, his conclusion that the new Minister had more "Genius than Ability" was not far from the mark. Believing it to be in the interest of the United States if Genet did not sail until conditions were more stable in France, Morris warned him of the hazards of a winter crossing. When he found Genet resolute, he gave the Minister a letter of introduction to Robert Morris (a distant cousin), perhaps in the hope that Robert Morris might be able to profit from the opportunity to sell supplies to Genet. The American Minister, however, did not entrust him with dispatches.[11]

Genet was in Rochefort by January 23, but contrary winds and storms detained the *Embuscade* for another month. Never a man to be idle, the Minister busied himself with a variety of matters, which, if not part of his duties, exhibited an exemplary sense of patriotism. Observing that the navy's failure to provide proper clothing for recruits was discouraging enlistments, he arranged for the local society of the Friends of Liberty to establish a fund for uniforms and contributed 300 livres to the enterprise. He also, as he proudly informed LeBrun, had been successful in preventing an incipient mutiny on the *Embuscade*. Not until February 20 did the *Embuscade* clear the harbor carrying on board the Minister, a great quantity of baggage ranging from carriages to a bidet, two secretaries of the legation (Pascal and Bournonville), his private secretary Moissonier, who had been with him in Russia, and two personal servants.[12] Just before he departed he received a packet of 250 blank military commissions, an indication of the size of the operation he was expected to mount to liberate Louisiana and Florida. He also learned from LeBrun that war had been declared against Great Britain on February 1 and that within a matter of weeks a similar challenge would be directed against Spain.

11. January 6, 1793, *Ibid.*, II, 595.

12. Genet to Le Brun, January 30, February 17, 1793, Genet Papers, LC. Date of his departure uncertain, but it was either February 17 or February 20 (the latter seems more likely). See Richard K. Murdoch, "The Genesis of the Genêt [*sic*] Schemes," *French American Review, II* (1949), 97, fn. 45.

4

American Politics: Spring 1793

IN THE FINAL DENOUEMENT of Genet's mission three factors seem most relevant: the nature of Girondin policy, the character of the Minister, and the political climate of the United States in the spring and summer of 1793. The first two (which have been considered in the previous chapters) provide the essential background for understanding Genet's demands and his reactions during his mission. It is equally important to examine in some detail the American political scene at the time of Genet's arrival, for the policy towards France worked out so laboriously by the Washington administration was not based on a calm and impartial analysis of national interest or binding treaty obligations. Instead it was forged in an atmosphere of intense and bitter political animosity within the inner circles of the administration and in the public arena. The Genet mission exposed, as no other previous episode, the extent and fury of the disagreement between the two groups which had been seeking to control national policy since the bitter controversy generated by the Hamiltonian fiscal program.[1]

At the time of Genet's arrival the exact nature and scope

1. On the general state of American politics in 1793 see: Malone, *Jefferson,* III; E. Noble Cunningham, *The Jeffersonian Republicans, 1789–1801* (University of North Carolina Press, 1957); Joseph Charles, *The Origins of the American Party System* (New York, 1961); Irving Brant, *James Madison: Father of the Constitution, 1787–1800* (Indianapolis, 1957).

of the political divisions within the United States was by no means clear to the public nor to the participants themselves. All recognized that there were two distinct groups or factions, one rallying about Secretary of the Treasury Alexander Hamilton, while the other looked to Congressman James Madison and Secretary of State Thomas Jefferson for leadership. As yet these two groups, which ultimately emerged as the Federalist and Republican parties, had neither a clearly defined membership nor a carefully articulated program. Indeed, it was not always possible to identify political figures with either faction, for many prominent men pursued an independent course. The only names applied to these factions (though Jefferson and his associates were using the phrase "republican interest" to describe themselves in 1792) were the terms of opprobium they used to label each other. Thus the Madison-Jefferson circle termed the Hamiltonians aristocrats, monocrats, monarchists, Tories, Anglomen, and without intending any flattery, the ministerial party.[2] The Hamiltonians, somewhat less inventive, had to be content with the application of such labels as mobocrats, or the democratical element. The issues raised by France's declaration of war on Great Britain in 1793 and the demands of Citizen Genet had a lasting effect on the rival factions. They were not transformed immediately into political parties but the controversy generated over the French Minister brought them out into the open, led to a more explicit declaration of principles, made it difficult for politicians to remain uncomitted, and, most importantly, compelled each to seek reinforcements by directly appealing to the people.

Until the spring of 1791 the conflict between the two factions had been a limited one, largely sectional in character with the Southerners functioning as the principal critics of the Hamiltonian program. The opposition had been centered in

2. Jefferson used the phrase "republican party" as early as May 23, 1792, in a letter to Washington. Worthington C. Ford, ed., *Writings of Thomas Jefferson* (10 vols., New York, 1892–99), VI, 3. [Hereinafter cited as Ford, *Jefferson*.]

the halls of Congress, where Madison emerged as the most effective leader of the forces attacking the fiscal program. Jefferson's leadership role at this time is somewhat difficult to define. Modern historians of the Washington administration are agreed that Madison deserves primary credit for mobilizing opposition to the fiscal policies of the Secretary of the Treasury. Jefferson remained in the background, yet in view of the close personal ties linking him with Madison, he was an important coadjutor. If he did not actively function as a leader, his advice was constantly sought and he fully supported the steps initiated by Madison.

During the early stages of the conflict over the Hamiltonian program, the participants tended to interpret their disagreement primarily in economic terms. Jefferson, who considered the fiscal policies of the Secretary of the Treasury destructive to his ideal of an agrarian republic, attributed these measures to the influence of the Eastern money men, stock jobbers, traders on British capital, and the "corrupt squadron" of paper men in Congress.[3] The controversy over the Bank of the United States early in 1791 by introducing the question of constitutionality stirred the public far more deeply than the previous measures, such as assumption of the state debts or the funding system.

At the same time that Madison was conducting his highly publicized Congressional opposition, Jefferson was waging quite a different campaign in the cabinet—less of a pitched battle than a series of skirmishes—over foreign policy. The cabinet struggle, known only to Madison and other intimates of the Secretary of State, centered around Hamilton's effort to prevent the President from approving policies which might be offensive to Great Britain. Hamilton, determined that nothing should interrupt Anglo-American commerce in view of the dependence of his fiscal program on tariff receipts, was particularly opposed to suggestions that the United States retaliate against Great Britain either through diplomatic channels or by means

3. Jefferson to Washington, May 23, 1792, *ibid.*, VI, 3ff.

of commercial reprisals. Jefferson objected to this submissive attitude which seemed tacitly to accept both British commercial discrimination and the violations of the Treaty of Peace of 1783. Moreover, he considered it grossly unjust to allow British merchants the same privileges as those extended to citizens of nations having commercial treaties with the United States. The Secretary of State was unaware of the full extent of Hamilton's activities, for he was ignorant of the confidential relationship established by the Secretary of the Treasury with British diplomatic agents, whom he kept informed of cabinet discussions.[4]

The continued success of the Hamiltonians in Congress led Madison (with Jefferson's approval) to take steps in 1791 to counteract the influence of the Secretary of the Treasury. First, the base of the opposition was broadened by seeking allies outside the South, particularly in New York State where there was a powerful anti-Hamiltonian faction headed by George Clinton, Aaron Burr, and Robert Livingston. The process by which these political alliances were established cannot be traced in detail, but the extent of the rapport can be measured by the fact that in 1792 the electoral votes of New York, Virginia, and North Carolina were cast for George Clinton for Vice President. Equally important was Madison's success in persuading his college classmate Philip Freneau, a successful propagandist of the American Revolution, to move to Philadelphia in the autumn of 1791 to launch a newspaper, the *National Gazette*. This move was designed to counter the influence of John Fenno's *Gazette of the United States,* whose columns were consistently filled with items favorable to the views of the Secretary of the Treasury. Freneau's enterprise, which Jefferson underwrote by granting him a State Department clerkship, was considered highly important, since provincial editors gathered national news exclusively by a scissors and paste operation on the Philadelphia press.

During the spring and summer of 1791 a new theme was

4. DeConde, *Entangling Alliance,* 74.

developed in the private correspondence of the Madison-Jefferson circle. While they continued to comment on the economic elements underlying Hamilton's plans, they now detected a far more sinister motive in the machinations of the Secretary of the Treasury and his friends—an attempt to subvert republican institutions and replace them with monarchical and aristocratic forms. The stake in the political conflict was not just the economic well-being of the farmers, so systematically ignored by Hamilton, but liberty itself was in jeopardy.

The convictions of the Madison-Jefferson circle were reinforced by the furore over Paine's *Rights of Man* published in the spring of 1791. Jefferson was inadvertently drawn into this controversy by the printer's inclusion in the preface of an extract from a letter written by the Secretary of State, praising Paine's work as a refutation of the "political heresies" which had sprung up in America. Jefferson also voiced his conviction that the citizens of the United States would "rally a second time round the standard of Common Sense." In the *Rights of Man,* which was a powerful response to Edmund Burke's much admired *Reflections on the French Revolution,* Paine maintained that the American and French Revolutions originated in a common set of principles. While American readers were not startled by this proposition, which they had taken for granted since 1789, many were shocked by Paine's insistence that the doctrine of the sovereignty of the people meant that the French nation embodied in the National Assembly had absolute power to reorganize the government of France. There were no restraints upon this authority, for, in Paine's opinion, the voice of the people was truly the voice of God. This argument ran counter to the American concept of a higher law as a limiting force on the popular will and also seemed to contradict the principle that a revolution was only justified when the compact had been violated.[5]

The *Rights of Man* stimulated anonymous commentators in the press. The most widely publicized critique was written

5. Malone, *Jefferson,* III, 354–59.

by John Quincy Adams under the pen name "Publicola"—essays at first attributed to his father. Although John Quincy Adams said much that was unfavorable about Burke, his condemnation of Paine, particularly his rejection of the contention that the people are absolutely sovereign, was much harsher. Publicola obviously feared that such doctrines, if accepted in America, might result in the kind of mob rule current in France. Today these essays scarcely seem to deserve Jefferson's conclusion that they were the work of a monarchist and Anglophile. Although Jefferson's fears about monarchy now appear excessive, there can be no doubt of the sincerity of his conviction. In 1791 anyone expressing misgivings about the French Revolution was automatically suspect in the eyes of the Secretary of State. Jefferson considered it highly significant that so many of Hamilton's supporters preferred Burke to Paine. The anxiety current in the Jefferson circle was unequivocally voiced by James Monroe in three essays signed "Aratus" appearing in Freneau's paper in November, 1791.[6] In these essays, Monroe, Jefferson's friend and confidant, not only voiced sympathy for French republicans but insisted that the fate of liberty in the United States was dependent upon the success of the Revolution in France.

It was at this time that Jefferson's apprehensions about the ultimate plans of the Hamiltonians led him to begin a record of notable events, conversations, and rumors, which reinforced his suspicions. Significantly he started this intermittent diary (known as the *Anas*) in August, 1971, by recording remarks made by the Secretary of the Treasury during a conversation about the political doctrines of John Adams. Hamilton told his colleague, although he would not let it be known publicly, that the "present govmnt. is not that which will answer the ends of society, by giving stability & protection to its rights, and that it will probably be found expedient to go to the British form." [7]

6. These essays are in the Philadelphia *National Gazette,* November 14, 24, December 12, 1791. On Monroe's authorship see Harry Ammon, *James Monroe: The Quest for National Identity* (New York, 1971), 87.

7. Jefferson, *Anas,* August 13, 1791, in Ford, *Jefferson,* I, 169.

Jefferson outlined his own position in some detail in a letter to Washington in May, 1792, in which he urged the President to run for a second term, since Washington's influence alone could prevent the "corrupt squadron" of speculators in bank stock and public securities from executing their plan of establishing a monarchy. Although the "republican party" desired to preserve the present form of government, it had not been as powerful in Congress as the "Monarchical federalists." Jefferson expected, however, that the approaching Congressional elections would alter the balance of power.[8] Washington also received a letter from Madison touching on many of the same points.

By a most remarkable coincidence, three days after Jefferson had unburdened himself to Washington, Hamilton wrote a lengthy letter (it runs to twenty pages in print) to Edward Carrington, Supervisor of the Revenue for Virginia. In bitter phrases Hamilton accused Jefferson, Madison, and their associates of leading a "faction hostile to me and my administration, and activated by views in my judgment subversive to the principles of good government and dangerous to the union, peace, and happiness of the Country." Not only were their views on foreign affairs "unsound & dangerous," but Madison and Jefferson cherished a "*womanish attachment to France and a womanish sentiment against Great Britain*. They would draw us into the closest embrace of the former & involve us in the consequences of her politics. . . ." If they were not restrained, Hamilton was certain they would involve the nation in a war with Great Britain within six months.[9] Hamilton's comments on the political principles of his rivals were rather vague in contrast to Jefferson's statements about the intentions of the Secretary of the Treasury. Only after the Jacobins seized power in June, 1793, did the Hamiltonians make an identification between the "republican interest" and the most radical ele-

8. *Ibid.*, VI, 1–4.

9. May 26, 1792, Harold C. Syrett, ed., *The Papers of Alexander Hamilton* (14 vols., New York, 1961–), XI, 429–39. The italics are in the original.

ment in French politics. In early 1792 Hamilton's primary concern was still with Jefferson's anti-British position.

The concern about the threat of monarchy was not reserved for private letters. Although the public at large does not seem to have been much stirred by this threat, the issue found its way into the press as the political essayists added this theme to their repertory. From time to time Congressional action reflected this new apprehension. In December, 1791, when Washington nominated Gouverneur Morris Minister to France, the Senate confirmed him reluctantly—the vote was sixteen to eleven. The general opinion of those in the negative was summed up by Senator James Monroe who objected to him as a "monarchy man" too deeply involved in speculative ventures to be suitable as a republican diplomat.[10] The fear of monarchy at times cropped up on the most unlikely occasions. During a House debate on the coinage in March, 1792, John Page of Virginia, who was closely allied to Jefferson, objected to using Washington's portrait on the coinage because it would constitute a "stamp of royalty." [11]

In the summer of 1792, Hamilton, determined to become the master of administration policy, moved to undermine the President's confidence in the Secretary of State and at the same time destroy Freneau, whose attacks constantly exasperated him. On July 25, after Washington and Jefferson had departed to Virginia for the summer, a letter written by Hamilton but signed "T.L." appeared in Fenno's *Gazette*. Under the veil of anonymity Hamilton charged Jefferson with granting Freneau a clerkship as a means of subsidizing attacks on the Washington administration. Further, he suggested that Jefferson himself had written for the *National Gazette*. During the next month under a variety of signatures, Hamilton alleged that Jefferson had opposed the federal Constitution and at one time had

10. Malone, *Jefferson,* II, 400.

11. Charles D. Hazen, *Contemporary American Opinion of the French Revolution* in Johns Hopkins University Studies in Historical and Political Science, Extra Vol. XVI (Baltimore, 1897), 151.

recommended the repudiation of the American debt to France. The last charge was completely false and the first fell short of the truth, for Jefferson had merely raised questions about certain provisions of the Constitution. Hamilton's accusations led to a lengthy controversy in the press with Madison and Monroe (as "Vindicator") assuming the burden of the defense. After failing to force Hamilton to admit he was the author of the attack, Monroe, in the last number, struck a personal note of the kind increasingly common in the next decade, when he hinted at damaging revelations which could be made if "T.L." revealed his name. Monroe was alluding to his recent discovery that Hamilton had been involved in an adulterous relationship with Mrs. Reynolds. Monroe and two other Congressmen had stumbled on this information while seeking evidence that the Secretary of the Treasury had been speculating in public securities.[12]

President Washington, naturally distressed at this airing of hostility between two of his cabinet members, attempted to close the breach. In this he met with little success, for both Jefferson and Hamilton were so convinced of the evil motives of the other that a reconciliation was out of the question. Hamilton could not accept the judgment of a person whose "principles of liberty" were equivalent to "principles of licentiousness," for this meant sacrificing "everything that is valuable and substantial in society to the vain reveries of a false and new-fangled philosophy." Nor could Jefferson trust a man whose "principles were adverse to liberty" and one who systematically undermined foreign policies presumably approved by the President.[13] When Jefferson and Hamilton returned to Philadelphia in the autumn, they maintained a formal courtesy, but clashed constantly in the cabinet. Again Washington appealed to Jefferson to "coalesce" with Hamilton behind administration policies, an action Jefferson deemed impossible. Neither could yield to the other without abandoning

12. Malone, *Jefferson,* II, 456–77.
13. Quoted in, *ibid.,* II, 465–67.

basic principles.[14] Considering their presence essential for his administration, Washington did not respond to Hamilton's suggestion that both resign.

The "republican interest" struck back at Hamilton in January, 1793, through resolutions sponsored by William Branch Giles, a Virginia Congressman on intimate terms with Madison and Jefferson. The inquiry into the Secretary's conduct of the Treasury provoked by Giles's proved rather disappointing, for no irregularities were uncovered. Hamilton's reports merely revealed several transactions, not illegal in themselves, which the Secretary would have preferred to conceal from the public. The debate on the Giles resolves left no doubt that the attack was leveled primarily against the Secretary himself and only secondarily at the fiscal system as a whole.[15]

During the winter of 1792–93 interest in the French Revolution increased, as public sympathy was stirred by the spectacle of France beleaguered by hostile monarchies. While some were distressed over the turmoil attending the destruction of the French monarchy, most accepted it as a necessary step. The September massacres did not receive as much notice in the press as might be expected, for the news of the victory of Valmy took precedence. Valmy was celebrated in America from Boston to Charleston with as much fervor as in France.[16]

Washington shared the current interest in the French Revolution. At first he approved, but as the violence increased, forcing his friend Lafayette into exile, the President became increasingly anxious about the outcome. These private misgivings did not at first affect official policy. Thus, when he learned in February, 1793, that the monarchy had been replaced by a republic, he approved Jefferson's note to Ternant assuring the French government that the "citizens of the United States . . . consider the union & pursuits between our two countries as a link which brings still closer their interests & affections. The genuine and general effusions of joy which . . .

14. Jefferson, *Anas,* February 7, 1793, Ford, *Jefferson,* I, 214–15.
15. Malone, *Jefferson,* III, 22–34.
16. Hazen, *Opinion of the French Revolution,* 164–69, 171, 246.

overspread our country on seeing the liberties of yours rise superior to foreign invasions & domestic troubles have proved . . . that our sympathies are great and sincere. . . ."[17] At the same time Washington instructed Morris to treat with officials of the Republic and authorized new advances on the French debt. The news of the King's execution, which reached America in March, noticeably changed Washington's attitude. Just before he left for Mount Vernon in March, 1793, when it was thought that Genet might arrive at any time, he instructed Jefferson to receive the Minister "without too much warmth or cordiality."[18] He was prepared to accept the Republic as the legal government, but he was not willing to let it seem that he approved of recent events in France.[19]

When Congress adjourned in March, 1793, the conflict between the two factions remained unresolved. Neither had made any significant gains over the previous year. In raising questions about Jefferson's associations with Freneau, Hamilton had embarrassed the Secretary of State, but he had not driven his colleague from the cabinet. Giles's attack had succeeded in doing nothing more than raising doubts about the propriety of Hamilton's loose interpretation of his authority as Secretary of the Treasury. The press had commented extensively on these issues and both sides had engaged in a minor pamphlet war, but the people, while interested, do not seem to have been deeply engaged in these controversies. Nor did these disputes have a noticeable impact on state political alignments. After two years of conflict, it cannot be said that public opinion was polarized in a distinct way. The struggle was still localized in the highest level of the national government—a battle which raged primarily in Congress and in the cabinet. Public men felt no compulsion to join sides. In a sense the political scene in the spring of 1793 could best be described

17. To Ternant, February 23, 1793, Ford, *Jefferson,* VI, 189–90.

18. *Anas,* March 30, 1793, *ibid.,* I, 224.

19. Douglas Southall Freeman, John Alexander Carroll and Mary Wells Ashworth, *George Washington* (7 vols., New York, 1948–57), VII, 25–30.

as a stalemate. The Genet mission altered this relationship drastically, bringing the parties out in the open, involving the public in an impassioned debate and creating an atmosphere in which political independence was no longer tolerated. Genet provided the issues needed to shift the two factions from dead center, and his activities constituted an essential step towards the formation of organized political parties by 1795.

5

American Neutrality Defined

ALTHOUGH THE *Embuscade,* which landed Genet at Charleston on April 8, 1793, was bound for Philadelpia, the Minister preferred to journey overland to the capital, sending his baggage and the legation secretaries by ship. Not only was he weary of the sea after a storm-wracked voyage lasting seven weeks, but he was naturally curious to have a first hand view of the nation which occupied a central role in French republican mythology. This decision had unfortunate consequences for the outcome of his mission. In the first place, it delayed his arrival in the capital until long after administration neutrality policy had been formulated. By lingering in the South, Genet lost whatever slight chance he may have had of influencing Washington's decisions concerning America's role as a neutral. Secondly, while in Charleston and totally ignorant of the administration position, he instituted measures to carry out his instructions. The steps he took led directly to his ultimate conflict with the President. Within a few days after his arrival, Genet commissioned four privateers. Christened most appropriately, *Republican, Anti-George, Sans-Culotte,* and—the finest touch of all—*Citizen Genet,* they were soon sending into Charleston English ships captured as prizes. The Minister also made the initial arrangements for an expedition to be launched against Spanish Florida. The details of this operation were entrusted to the French Consul, Michel Ange Mangourit, whose patriotism met Genet's approval.[1]

1. See Keller, "Genet Mission," 112–28; Boston *Columbian Centinel,*

Acting on the assumption that the enthusiasm of his public reception was a precise indication of the tone of the national administration, Genet saw no reason to postpone the execution of his instructions until his official reception. He also found considerable encouragement in the friendliness of state officials and distinguished local citizens. Immediately after his arrival he called on Governor William Moultrie who saw no impropriety in Genet's plan to issue letters of marque to privateers. It seemed eminently logical to Moultrie, who was a veteran of the American Revolution, that France should be accorded the same privileges she had granted Americans during their struggle for independence. Moreover, the federal government had not issued any directives to the contrary. The Governor was equally accommodating when Genet broached the possibility of organizing an expedition to liberate Spanish Florida. Like many South Carolinians, Moultrie had frontier land claims whose value would be enhanced if Spain were eliminated from Florida. Moultrie recommended men (including his private secretary, Stephen Drayton), whom Genet might enlist in the enterprise. Apparently Genet's projects were also approved by some of the leading citizens of the state. During the ten days that he lingered in Charleston, the Minister was entertained by General Thomas Pinckney, Christopher Gadsden, John Rutledge, Aedanus Burke, and by two leading figures whom he had met many years before at his father's home—Ralph Izard and Alexander Gillon. It is not surprising that after a week in Charleston he was in an euphoric mood, writing LeBrun that the fervor of his public reception had not only routed the pro-English party but established beyond doubt that the American people were ready to succour their brothers across the Atlantic.[2]

Not until April 18 did Genet leave for Philadelphia riding in his carriage drawn by four sturdy horses purchased from General Pinckney.[3] On the very same day President Washing-

---

May 1, 4, 11, 1793; Philadelphia *Dunlap's American Advertiser,* April 22, 1793; Minnigerode, *Jefferson,* 185–81; Woodfin, "Genet," 185–91.

2. Genet to LeBrun, April 16, 1793, Turner, *CFM,* II, 211–13.

3. Thomas Pinckney to Genet, April 19, 1793, Genet Papers, LC.

ton sat down with his cabinet in Philadelphia to begin a series of conferences to define the course of the administration. The President had cut short his vacation at Mount Vernon to return to the capital as soon as he learned that France had declared war on Great Britain. During the early stages of the war, when Austria and Prussia had been the only powers opposing France, there had been no need to evaluate the position of the United States. England's participation, however, made basic policy decisions imperative, for the war would now spread to the seas exposing American shipping to new hazards. Moreover, it was also necessary to consider the extent to which the territorial guarantee in the Treaty of Alliance of 1778 would be operative. The President, who was unaware that Genet had landed when he began the cabinet discussions, was naturally anxious to resolve the major issues before the Minister appeared in Philadelphia.

There had been some inconclusive discussions about Franco-American relations after John Adams's son-in-law, William S. Smith, arrived in Philadelphia in February bearing a letter from the French Foreign Minister to Washington. As the holder of a contract as a French purchasing agent, Smith had been authorized to request advances on the debt. Before leaving Paris, he had had a private interview with Brissot, and consequently was able to inform Washington that the Girondins were ready to negotiate a broad commercial agreement and that they intended sponsoring movements to liberate Louisiana and other Spanish possessions. Smith also told the President of the Girondin resentment over the conduct of Gouveneur Morris. The President had been aware of the friction between Morris and the Girondins through complaints registered by Ternant and from Morris's letters, but only now did he understand the seriousness of the disagreement. After consulting his secretaries about Smith's request for an advance on the debt, Washington decided to refuse, since payments were already being made to Ternant. He also discussed the question of replacing Morris, but the point was still unsettled when he left for Mount Vernon in March. In view of the disturbed conditions in France, the President's reaction to the suggestion of a commercial treaty was negative. Smith's information led to only one significant action: the Secretary of State wrote the American commissioners negotiating in Madrid, cautioning them not to enter into any agreements involving a mutual guarantee of territories in return for the opening of the Mississippi. The commissioners were given no explanation of this order other than that the United States wished to remain uncommitted.[4]

In the spring of 1793 basic policy towards France was shaped more by the Secretary of the Treasury, whose influence over the President seemed unshakeable, than by the Secretary of State. Hamilton was absolutely determined that nothing should be done which might directly benefit France (and thereby offend England). Well aware of popular sympathy for France, he chose to advocate a policy of neutrality so rigid that France would be denied the special benefits she might normally expect as an ally. On April 9, just a few days after he notified Washington of the French declaration of war against England, Hamilton wrote his confidant, Chief Justice John Jay, asking him to draft a proclamation of neutrality. This the Justice obligingly did, and his draft formed the substructure of the President's subsequent proclamation. The principal difference between the two was that the final document omitted the sections in Jay's version which had reflected unfavorably upon recent events in France and questioned the stability of the new regime. So certain was Hamilton of presidential concurrence that he at once informed the British Minister, George Hammond, that Washington, while admitting the validity of the treaties of 1778, would follow a policy of strict neutrality, refusing to form new agreements with France until a durable government had been installed.[5]

How well Hamilton prepared the ground for the cabinet discussions can be seen from the questions which Washington

4. Freeman, *Washington,* VII, 29–33.

5. Keller, "Genet Mission," 54–73; DeConde, *Entangling Alliance,* 72–73, 86–87; Hammond to Grenville, April 2, 1793, Great Britain, Public Records Office, Foreign Affairs, Photostats, Library of Congress.

sent his secretaries for consideration at the first meeting on April 19. These queries, as Jefferson noted, bore every evidence of Hamilton's hand. Although the President submitted thirteen questions they can be summed up much more succinctly: Shall the President issue a proclamation of neutrality? Shall he receive Genet? If he is received, should it be with reservations? Is the Treaty of Alliance of 1778 negotiated with Louis XVI still in effect now that the monarchy has been abolished? Shall Congress be called into special session?

There was little discussion about the proposal that Congress be summoned, for all agreed that this would unnecessarily alarm the country. As far as Jefferson was concerned there was little advantage for the republican interest in convening a legislative body with a pro-administration bias. In all probability, Hamilton deliberately introduced the question about receiving Genet to distract Jefferson from other issues and offer a point on which a concession could be made. After all Washington had previously decided that the Minister should be received without reservation.

The proposal that the President issue a proclamation of neutrality produced an extensive controversy. It was not that Jefferson objected to neutrality, for he opposed measures tending to draw the nation into the war, but he objected to the idea of a public pronouncement. In the first place, he deemed it foolish to proclaim neutrality as an official policy without first obtaining something in exchange from the belligerents. Secondly, he questioned the constitutionality of the action. He argued (and with this Madison concurred) that a proclamation amounted in effect to an invasion of the Congressional power to declare war. To assert that the nation was at peace deprived the legislature of its authority in this area. In raising these objections Jefferson stood alone. Hamilton, Secretary of War Henry Knox, and Attorney General Edmund Randolph all agreed that such a pronouncement was an executive act within the power of the President. At Washington's request Randolph drew up a proclamation, but before it was issued on April 22 the word "neutrality" was deleted in response to Jefferson's protests. The Secretary of State considered the omission of this one word a substantial victory, but in truth it did not alter the obvious intent of the proclamation which warned the people to refrain from acts hostile to either belligerent, for the nation was at peace with both. Citizens aiding or abetting hostilities against either power rendered themselves liable to punishment. Washington's action established a lasting precedent vastly extending the power of the executive branch of the government.[6]

After a second cabinet meeting failed to reach a conclusion about the validity of the Treaty of Alliance of 1778, Hamilton and Jefferson submitted written opinions. Both secretaries accepted the premise that the United States should not become involved in the war, but on all other points they were at odds. The Secretary of the Treasury insisted that the treaty must be considered of questionable validity, since it had been negotiated with a ruler subsequently repudiated. Therefore, he proposed it be suspended until a legitimate government had been established in France. In the meantime Genet should be given a conditional reception. Jefferson, adhering to established international usage, pointed out that treaties were made between nations and not between rulers. Consequently, the treaty was still in effect. Since it seemed quite unlikely that France would invoke the mutual territorial guarantee, why not, he asked, wait until the administration learned of France's intentions before defining policy. There was, in his opinion, no basis upon which France could invoke this clause, for the treaty was defensive in character, whereas in this case France was the aggressor against England. He also feared that premature action might offend France and invite retaliation. Was not "an injured friend the bitterest of foes. . . ?" The reception of Genet implied nothing beyond a *de facto* recognition of the government in power. Concurring with Jefferson's arguments Washington did not alter his plan to receive the Minister and left the treaty question for future determination. Any other

6. DeConde, *Entangling Alliance,* 186–87; Freeman, *Washington,* VII, 45–50; Malone, *Jefferson,* III, 68–72.

course would have contradicted his earlier decisions, for he had in effect recognized the Republic when he instructed Morris to continue to deal with the new regime.[7]

These cabinet meetings, typical of dozens during the next four months, nakedly revealed the intense disagreement between Jefferson and Hamilton. Only now did the President comprehend the extent of their hostility. The disharmony in the administration was painful to Washington, not only for personal reasons, but because it compounded the difficulty of reaching policy decisions. He considered it essential (since the two secretaries reflected and could influence powerful segments of opinion) to formulate policies which would be acceptable to each, satisfy his own concept of national welfare, and not be out of harmony with public sentiment. His struggle to create unity within the administration led him to depart from his usual practice of requesting written opinion from the secretaries in favor of frequent cabinet meetings. In these sessions the alignment of forces rarely changed. Hamilton was invariably supported by Knox, whom Jefferson considered a feeble echo of the Secretary of the Treasury. Attorney General Randolph, attached to the President by ties of friendship and yet aware of the intense pro-French feeling in Virginia, vainly sought to act as a moderating influence. Jefferson, hoping for an ally in Randolph, was both irritated and distrustful over his colleague's conduct. Randolph, he concluded, was but a chameleon taking the color most pleasing to the President. This may seem a harsh judgment, but as other episodes in his career indicate, Randolph was inclined to vacillate. Throughout the tedious and frequently acrimonious exchanges in the cabinet, Washington, except for one occasion, managed to control his temper. In the end he adopted a course not entirely pleasing to either Hamilton or Jefferson. Both could only grudgingly admit that it was a fair neutrality, which was not quite what either wanted.[8]

7. DeConde, *Entangling Alliance*, 190–97.

8. Malone, *Jefferson,* III, 68–131; Freeman, *Washington,* VII, 46–125.

Jefferson had failed to prevent the issuance of the President's proclamation, but he felt he had made some gains during the cabinet sessions. He had at least kept out the word neutrality (a point he overstressed), he had prevented the suspension of the Treaty of Alliance, and he had blocked the attempt to receive Genet conditionally. He considered this "fair neutrality" as necessary "to keep out the calamities of war," although, as he confessed to Madison, he knew that it would "prove a disagreeable pill to our friends." [9] By a fair neutrality, Jefferson anticipated a neutral stance which would permit France all benefits possible while denying them to the British. He wished a benevolent neutrality of the kind then practiced by the European powers. The proclamation issued by the President was phrased in such a way that it could be given a pro-French or a pro-British direction. The key figure in its application was the President, whose prestige was so great, as Jefferson was aware, that the people would willingly approve any course he chose. "If anything," Jefferson observed to Madison, "prevents it from being a mere English neutrality, it will be that the penchant of the P. is not that way, and above all, the ardent spirit of our constituents." [10] In view of Hamilton's obvious ascendancy over the President, Jefferson felt that public opinion must be brought to bear on the President to convince him that people were unshakably pro-French and anti-British. Fortunately the arrival of Genet offered the perfect opportunity. The French Minister would "furnish the occasion for the people to testify their affections without the cold caution of the government." [11]

A few days after writing this letter Jefferson was heartened by the reception given the *Embuscade* in Philadelphia as she entered the harbor with her prizes. As the vessels came into view, "thousands & thousands of the *yeomanry* of the city crowded & covered the wharves. Never before was such a

9. To Madison, April 28, 1793, Ford, *Jefferson,* VI, 232.
10. May 12, 1793, *ibid.,* VI, 251.
11. To Madison, April 28, 1793, *ibid.,* VI, 232.

crowd seen there, and when the British colors were seen *reversed* & the French flying above them they burst into peals of exultation." What a happy contrast, he told Monroe, to the attitude of Hamilton and his friends, who were "panic-struck if we refuse our breach to every kick which Gr Brit. may chuse to give it." [12]

The public turnout for Genet on his leisurely journey northward was everything Jefferson desired. At every town he was greeted by citizen delegations and presented with florid addresses praising liberty and expressing gratitude for France's past aid. American enthusiasm for the French Revolution was undeniable, but, as Genet failed to note, none of the addresses promised anything beyond sympathy. The only suggestion of a more active role came in the form of proposals in the press that subscriptions be taken to purchase supplies for France. It is true that Genet was deluged with offers of vast quantities of flour by American merchants, but with the understanding that France would pay for them. At the receptions and dinners honoring him, Genet made a fine impression with his informality, his evident liking for everything he saw, and his ability to respond in English to the addresses.[13] Detained by civic celebrations his pace was slow until he reached Richmond. Here, after seeing the President's proclamation, he declined an invitation to a public dinner and pressed on to Philadelphia.

Most of those who met the Minister were favorably impressed—at least by external appearances. John Steele, a not overly friendly observer who encountered him in Salisbury, North Carolina, reported to Hamilton that Genet had "a good person, a fine ruddy complection [*sic*], quite active and always seems in a bustle." In his opinion Genet behaved "more like a busy man than a man of business," who would try to "laugh us into war, if he can." Steele also noted that the Minister, like so

12. To Monroe, May 5, 1793, *ibid.,* VI, 238. Italics are in the original.

13. Quote is from Philadelphia *Dunlap's American Advertiser,* May 30, 1793; on his journey see Keller, "Genet Mission," 124–29; Woodfin, "Genet," 176–79.

many Europeans, had a very mistaken notion about the "penetration and knowledge of the people." [14] From Baltimore, James Iredell reported that Genet was a "handsome man, with a fine open countenance and pleasing and unaffected manners." [15] The reaction of those committed to the cause of France was strongly positive. John Dawson, a Virginian allied to Jefferson and Madison, had nothing but praise: "He appears to be a man possessed of much information, added to the most engaging & agreeable manners that I ever saw, he is very easy, communicative & dignified & will precisely suit the taste of our countrymen—all who have seen him are delighted. . . ." [16]

While Genet was savoring the adulation of the public, the issues raised by the outbreak of war between France and England led to further clashes between Hamilton and Jefferson. In the absence of machinery to enforce neutrality, Hamilton suggested that the collectors of the revenue, the only federal officials in the major ports, be authorized to report violations to him. Jefferson was outraged at the creation of a "corps of spies or informers against their fellow citizens" reporting directly to the Secretary of the Treasury. He recommended that enforcement be entrusted to the War Department or preferably to state authorities. Regarding Hamilton's plan as a slight on the office of the Attorney General, Jefferson sought Randolph's support. The Attorney General, unwilling to oppose the use of the collectors, obtained Hamilton's consent that they should report to state governors and district attorneys. Jefferson's partial victory endured only a few months. As state authorities proved incapable of checking violations, the President agreed in August that the collectors should submit evidence of violations to the federal attorneys, thus placing the responsibility for enforcement on the federal government.[17]

Two weeks before Genet reached Philadelphia, the admin-

14. April 30 [1793], Syrett, *Hamilton Papers,* XIV, 359.
15. Quoted in Hazen, *French Revolution,* 274, fn. 1.
16. To Madison, quoted in Woodfin, "Genet," 126.
17. Quote is from Jefferson to Edmund Randolph, May 8, 1793, Ford, *Jefferson,* VI, 245–46. See also Jefferson, *Anas,* May 6–7, 1793, *ibid.,* I, 269–70, and Malone, *Jefferson,* III, 84–86.

istration was presented with the first practical test of neutrality, when the British Minister challenged the legality of the capture of the *Grange*, an English ship taken prize by the *Embuscade* in Delaware Bay. Although Jefferson had shared the rejoicing over British humiliation as the *Grange* entered the Philadelphia harbor flying French colors, he accepted without hesitation the ruling of the Attorney General that she had been captured in American waters and requested her release. Genet honored this ruling two days after his arrival in the capital, an event noteworthy in itself as the only occasion on which he fully complied with American protests about French violations of neutrality.[18]

As Genet neared Philadelphia in mid-May, the members of the republican interest were planning a welcome calculated to put previous receptions in the shadow.[19] The intent of the Philadelphia reception was somewhat different from those organized elsewhere in the country. The earlier demonstrations had been spontaneous expressions of friendship for France and sympathy for the Revolution. They had not been arranged to influence American policy or as a commentary upon the political divisions within the administration. The reception planned for Philadelphia, however, was intended to impress upon the President the intensity of public affection for France and at the same time demonstrate the strength of native republicanism. It was a strictly partisan affair. The arrangements were in the hands of prominent Philadelphians of an anti-Hamilton persuasion—David Rittenhouse, President of the American Philosophical Society, Alexander J. Dallas, Secretary of State of Pennsylvania, Jonathan Dickinson Sergeant, one of the great lawyers of the day, Peter S. Duponceau, a former aid on Baron von Steuben's staff and now a leading member of the bar, and Charles Biddle, a member of one of the city's wealthiest families. Hamilton, as he observed their activities, struck

18. Malone, *Jefferson,* 81–83.

19. On his reception in Philadelphia see *ibid.,* III, 92–95; Keller, "Genet Mission," 142–59; *Dunlap's American Advertiser* May 18, 1793; Boston *Columbian Centinel,* May 19, 1793; New York *Daily Advertiser,* May 23, 1793.

them off as "men who have been uniformly the enemies" of the administration.[20] Their plans were thrown momentarily into confusion when Genet slipped into town on May 16 by different road from that on which he had been expected. Consequently the crowd which had been awaiting him could not greet him as planned. In the evening a meeting of citizens prepared an address to be presented to the Minister on the seventeenth. Hamilton's friends were not inactive. On the afternoon of the sixteenth they called a meeting of merchants to prepare an address to the President endorsing the proclamation of neutrality and urging strict enforcement. This was presented to Washington the next day.

The public reception for Genet took place on May 17 when Biddle and Rittenhouse heading a select committee of thirty and followed, according to Jefferson, by "a vast concourse" of citizens marched to the Minister's lodgings at the City Hotel. Estimates of the size of the crowd which gathered around the hotel varied according to political opinion. Jefferson gave a figure of 1,000, while Hamilton thought it was no larger than five or six hundred. Later Genet inflated it to 6,000. Entering the Minister's room the committee presented an address, which acknowledged the nation's "obligations" and "attachment" to France—"our first and best ally"—and affirmed the exultation of all Americans over France's continued success in the war. Ever fluent, Genet replied extemporaneously, asking that the "sincerity of his sentiments" excuse his faulty English. Then in the "most pathetick tones" (according to the press account), he told how deeply his emotions had been stirred by the discovery of the devotion of the people to the cause of liberty. Turning to the subject of his mission, he announced, since there should be no secrets between republics, that France did not expect the United States to enter the war. This news was pleasing, but his next words were prophetic of the misunderstandings which lay ahead. France, he continued, "remembering that she has already combatted for your liberties—and if it was necessary, and she had the power, would again enlist in your cause,

20. Alexander Hamilton to ______________, [May 18, 1793], Syrett, *Hamilton Papers,* XIV, 474.

we hope, and everything I hear and see assures me our hope will be realized, that her citizens will be treated as brothers in danger, and distress." After he completed his remarks to the committee which hailed them with "shouts and salutations," he went to the window and addressed "a few but emphatick sentences" to the throng in the street.[21]

For the next few weeks Genet lived, to use his own description, in the midst of "perpetual fêtes." Delegations of citizens and representatives of organizations such as the French Benevolent Society (a Santo Domingan refugee organization) and the German Republican Society (the first of the Democratic Republican societies formed on the model of the French political clubs) called to present addresses. On the evening of Saturday the eighteenth, the same day as his official reception by the President, he was entertained at a "Republican Dinner" organized by French residents in Philadelphia. Among the guests were the officers of the *Embuscade* and Ternant, whom Genet considered acceptably republican. As befitted a French patriotic celebration the table was decorated with a liberty tree and the guest took turns wearing a liberty cap supplied by the managers. After the Minister's secretary sang the "Marseillaise" the Minister enchanted the guests with a "truly patriotic and republican" song rendered with "great energy and judgement" to a tune from an operetta by Renaud d'Ast. The last verse, as translated by a guest, aptly expressed the mood of the guests:

> Liberty! liberty, be thy name adored forever,
> Tyrants beware! your tott'ring thrones must fall;
> Our int'rest links the free together,
> And Freedom's sons are Frenchmen all.

21. Boston *Columbian Centinel,* May 29, 1793; Jefferson to Madison, May 19, 1793, Ford, *Jefferson,* VI, 260. There seems to be no basis for the rather fantastic statement made many years later by John Adams that after Genet's arrival "ten thousand people" roamed the streets of Philadelphia day after day and threatened "to drag Washington out of his house and effect a revolution in the government or compel it to declare war in favor of the French Revolution. . . ." The government was only saved, according to Adams, by the outbreak of yellow fever in the late summer. John Adams to Jefferson, June 30, 1813, quoted in DeConde, *Entangling Alliance,* 306.

A few days later the officers of the *Embuscade* returned the compliment entertaining on board a large company including Governor Thomas Mifflin of Pennsylvania, Secretary of War Henry Knox, and William S. Smith.[22]

The festivities reached a climax on June 1 when 200 guests, paying the substantial tariff of four dollars, attended a dinner at Oeller's Hotel. It was an elaborate function graced by an artillery battery which fired fifteen rounds at the conclusion of the first, eighth, and last toasts, and three after all the others. The toasts rang the changes on liberty, republicanism and the cause of France. The fifteenth and last toast was typical: "May the clarion of Freedom sounded by France awaken the people of the World to their own happiness, and the Tyrants of the Earth be prostrated by its triumphant sounds." Again Genet displayed his vocal talent by singing the "Marseillaise" in French after which Duponceau repeated it in English. Freneau contributed a new patriotic song to the tune of "God Save the King" now transformed into "God Save the Rights of Man." The final verses must have indeed been pleasing to the French Minister.

> Hail, hail! Columbia's sons,
> The cause of France is thine
> With you she fought and bled,
> Those Laurels to entwine.
> Hence let our ev'ry action show,
> We feel her joys, we feel her woe.
>
> Rejoice ye Patriot sons,
> With festive mirth and glee
> Let all join hands around the cap of Liberty
> And in full chorus join the song
> May France ne'er want a WASHINGTON.[23]

What did all this mean? Did the guests take these words literally, or did they, as Charles Biddle asserted years later, look upon songs as "truly ridiculous"?[24] They were unques-

22. New York *Daily Advertiser,* May 23, 1793.
23. Philadelphia *Dunlap's American Advertiser,* May 28, June 1, 4, 1793.
24. Quoted in Minnigerode, *Jefferson,* 216.

tionably expressions of a deeply and genuinely felt emotion, but they were not, as Genet thought, an incitement to action. Without the slightest understanding of American politics, Genet, weighing these effusions in the light of current French practices, interpreted them as indicating an intention to support France—an indication so powerful that the American government could not ignore these demonstrations unless it were prepared to embark upon a despotic course. Therefore, when the Washington administration failed to agree with his interpretation of America's treaty obligations, he looked upon this action as a violation of the express will of the people. Under these circumstances he believed it his duty not only to France but to the cause of free government in America to rally the people against the administration. It was never easy for Genet to admit that he had erred. Consequently, some years later, when he commented on the events of 1793, he blamed Jefferson and the Republicans for his misunderstanding. They had, he insisted, systematically deceived him and used him for their own purposes.[25]

As much as Genet relished public ceremonials not all invitations were acceptable. He refused to attend a dinner of the Society of the Cincinnati because the Vicomte de Noailles, an émigré who had served under Washington in the Continental army, would be present. Genet erroneously believed that Noailles was a secret emissary from French royalists seeking American support. After his rupture with the administration he made much of the fact that the President had received the vicomte, but he overlooked the fact that the reception had been unofficial. Washington had greeted Noailles privately as an old comrade-in-arms.[26]

The extent of Genet's habit of substituting the rhetoric of public demonstrations for the reality of diplomacy is evidenced by the fact that in the three dispatches he sent LeBrun during his first two months in America he made only a passing refer-

25. Genet to Jefferson, July 4, 1797, letter not sent, reproduced in *ibid.*, 418.

26. Hazen, *French Revolution,* 184.

ence to his official presentation to the President and said nothing at all about his conferences with the Secretary of State. He thought it sufficient to inform LeBrun on May 31 that the people of America had risen to acknowledge him as the Minister of the Republic. The "voice of the people" had sufficed to nullify the proclamation of neutrality. He promised LeBrun that his mission would succeed not because of the cooperation of public officials, but because he had the endorsement of the people.[27] These dispatches, which contained no solid information about the state of the relations between the two countries, were so unsatisfactory that Deforgues (LeBrun's successor) preemptorily demanded specific details.[28]

Genet was presented to Washington by the Secretary of State on the afternoon of May 18. If the interview, conducted in the formal manner preferred by the President, displeased the French Minister, he said nothing to that effect in a dispatch written the same day. It was only later, in face of the administration's rigid neutrality, that he interpreted Washington's formality as hostility towards France. Not until October, after he learned that his recall had been requested, did he describe his reception as "cold" and assert that the presence of medallion portraits of the "family Capet" in the President's room had been a calculated offense.[29]

From Genet's infrequent allusions in his dispatches and the occasional comments in Jefferson's letters, it is possible to gather in a general way something of the character of their early association. Everything predisposed each to be drawn to the other. Idolizing Jefferson as a demigod of the revolutionary movement which had shaken two continents, Genet assumed that his requests would be readily honored by a man who was not only frankly sympathetic toward the cause of France but who was also a friend of leading Girondins—Condorcet, Bris-

27. Turner, *CFM,* II, 216.

28. Minister of Foreign Affairs to Genet, July 30, 1793, *ibid.,* II, 228–31.

29. Genet to LeBrun, June 19, October 7, 1793, *ibid.*, II, 217, 244ff; Freeman, *Washington,* VII, 72–75.

sot, and Clavière. In the early stages of their relationship Genet had no reason to modify the opinion expressed before their first meeting, when he wrote that Jefferson's "principles, talents, and devotion to the cause of liberty" made him certain of the complete success of his mission.[30] Jefferson, who was ready to approve any Minister sent by the Republic, found this witty, seemingly well-informed, and ingratiating young diplomat much to his liking. His pleasure in welcoming Genet was all the greater when he learned directly from the Minister that France, instead of invoking the territorial guarantee, was prepared to negotiate a generous commercial agreement. He voiced his relief and pleasure after his first meeting with Genet in a letter to Madison: "It is impossible for anything to be more affectionate, more magnanimous than the purport of his mission. . . . In short he offers everything & asks nothing." [31] During Genet's first month in Philadelphia their association was an agreeable one, both in official conferences and on the many occasions when the French Minister visited Jefferson at his summer home a few miles from the city on the banks of the Schuylkill.

It was a good beginning, but as Jefferson was aware, there were serious disappointments in store for the French Minister. Even the Secretary of State could not gauge their exact extent, for the cabinet was still debating measures necessary to implement the proclamation, for which there were no American precedents. European usages provided no real guidance, nor were writers on international law helpful. Prior to Genet's reception only one major decision had been reached, namely, that the outfitting of French armed vessels in American ports was contrary to a policy of strict neutrality and was not required under the terms of the Treaty of Commerce and Amity. The Secretary of State knew, of course, that Washington was unwilling to conclude a new treaty with France in spite of the proferred commercial advantages. Washington thought it unwise (and his reluctance was reinforced by Hamilton's arguments)

30. To LeBrun May 18, 1793, Turner, *CFM,* II, 215.
31. May 19, 1793, Ford, *Jefferson,* VI, 260–61.

to enter into long-term agreements in view of the political instability of France. Jefferson did not take issue with this conclusion, for he agreed that the "internal combustion" within France made such arrangements uncertain. For much the same reason the President had determined not to make large advances on the debt owed France. On this point Jefferson would have preferred a more lenient policy, but Hamilton was adamantly opposed.[32]

Recent news from France increased the feeling of uncertainty about the future of the republican government. In the weeks before Genet reached Philadelphia, the press carried stories about the royalist uprising under way in the Vendée, the riots in Paris in early March which had resulted in the destruction of a number of Girondin presses, and, most alarming, the report that French armies were being driven out of Belgium and Holland. This was capped (just as Genet arrived in the capital) by the news that Dumouriez, the hero of Valmy and commander of the French armies in Holland, had deserted and taken refuge with the allies.

Still, no matter what upheavals might yet occur in France, it was essential for Jefferson's purpose to avoid friction with America's ally. He never doubted that in the event of a rupture with France the Hamiltonians would seize the occasion to initiate a rapprochement with Great Britain and take the country another step along the road to monarchy. As he told Madison after his first conference with Genet, Hamilton and his friends, "under pretense of avoiding war on the one side have no great antipathy to run foul of it on the other, and to make a party in the confederacy of princes against human liberty."[33] Jefferson's only hope was that continued manifestations of pro-French sentiment (which also meant pro-republican) would give a decisive turn to national policy. With developments up to the time of Genet's reception he was well satisfied. "Parties," he told Monroe on June 4, "seem to have

32. Quote is from Jefferson to Madison, June 2, 1793, Ford, *Jefferson,* VI, 278.
33. May 19, 1793, *ibid.,* VI, 261.

taken a very well defined form in this quarter. The old tories, joined by our merchants who trade on British capital, paper dealers, and the idle rich of the great commercial towns are with the kings. All other descriptions with the French. The war has kindled & brought forward the two parties with an ardour which our interests merely, could never excite. I pray that the events of the summer may not damp the spirit of our approaching Congress to whom we look forward to give the last direction to the government in which we are embarked." [34]

It is clear from everything Jefferson wrote in the spring of 1793 that he believed the current political tensions could only be resolved in Congress. Public opinion was an important factor in his thinking, but it was a force which only worked effectively through existing governmental institutions. Here he differed radically from Genet whose French background led him to regard public sentiment as the determining element in the political process and one directly operative upon the government itself. It is not surprising that Jefferson should have emphasized the central role of Congress. He was the republican spokesman in the cabinet, but he was blocked at every turn by Hamilton. In the past the most effective, if not invariably successful, opposition to Hamiltonian policies had been mounted in Congress with full publicity (in contrast to the secrecy of cabinet debates) by Madison, Monroe, William Branch Giles, and others of a republican persuasion. The outbreak of war between France and England, which precipitated the first major crisis to face the Washington administration when Congress was not in session, presented a difficult problem. Although it would take a greater force than Jefferson could muster in the cabinet to counter the pro-British orientation of American foreign policy so vigorously pushed by Hamilton, he opposed suggestions that Congress be called in session because he could see no advantage in summoning a body which had been dominated by the Hamiltonians. He could

34. *Ibid.,* VI, 281–82, and also Jefferson to Madison, June 29, 1793, when he speaks of the war as bringing out the "Republicans & Monocrats" in force, *ibid.,* VI, 326.

only hope that the pro-French spirit of the people would have a sufficient effect on Congressional elections to return legislators of a republican stamp.

What did he expect the next session to achieve in a positive way? Unfortunately he never elaborated on this subject beyond general comments such as that made to Harry Innes late in May: "This summer is of immense importance to the future of mankind all over the earth, and not a little so to ours. For tho' its issue should not be marked by a direct change in our constitution, it will influence the tone & principles of its administration as to lead it to something very different in the one event from what it would be in the other." [35] A republican majority would restrain further projects of the Secretary of the Treasury and also prevent the enactment of measures slanting neutrality in a pro-British direction. Obviously Jefferson expected the President, who was sensitive to public opinion, to take his cue from Congress.

The execution of Jefferson's strategy required time to let public opinion slowly take effect. The success of his plan depended upon a large degree of forebearance on the part of the French Minister, who would have to postpone the realization of some of the objects of his mission for six months. In view of the rebuffs which Jefferson knew to be in store for Genet, the Secretary of State resorted to the dangerous expedient of establishing a personal rapport with the French Minister. It was important that Genet understand fully the domestic political situation and conduct himself in a way to foster the interests of the republican and pro-French factions. Taking the Minister into his confidence, he explained the conflict within the administration, making it clear that the disagreement reflected much larger issues than the definition of neutrality—it was essentially a struggle in which the stakes were monarchy or republicanism. The issue could only be resolved by Congress, for this body alone had the power to block the Hamiltonians. Consequently, Jefferson counseled Genet to be patient, for republican

35. May 23, 1793, *ibid.*, VI, 266.

forces would surely triumph.[36] Genet listened to the Secretary and raised no objections, but there can be no doubt that his understanding of the situation was quite different from Jefferson's. When Jefferson spoke of monarchists and the pro-British faction, Genet thought in terms of counter-revolutionaries and traitors. The comments of the Secretary upon the power of public opinion were automatically translated into the concept of the sovereignty of the people. This misunderstanding was serious, for it led Genet to conclude that he must take an activist role to guarantee the triumph of the republicans in America. As the French Consul in New York commented in November, Genet acted as if he were in France and failed to understand that "in the United States one can belong to [either] of two parties without running the risk of being hung, or even of being disgraced." [37]

Jefferson's advice might have been heeded by a less impulsive and self-confident diplomat, or one who was less desperate to report positive results to his superiors. The summer was indeed a critical one, but not quite in the way Jefferson expected. Although the parties were more sharply delineated than ever before, the hoped-for republican triumph was still seven years distant.

36. Genet to Jefferson, July 4, 1797, letter not sent, in Minnigerode, *Jefferson,* 418; Genet to Minister of Foreign Affairs, July 31, Ford, *Jefferson,* I, 246, fn. 1.

37. Hauterive, MS Journal, November 5, 1793, New-York Historical Society.

6

Neutrality Challenged

CITIZEN GENET began the formal business of his mission with a proposal designed by the Girondins as the best means of inaugurating a new era in the relations between the two nations and at the same time set an example to the world of the fraternal bond uniting all free peoples. He proposed that the United States, in response to the liberal grant of trading privileges made by the National Convention, enter into a treaty establishing a "true family compact" uniting the two powers in the most intimate bonds. The offer was presented with rhetorical flourishes so dear to his French contemporaries and not entirely without appeal for Americans:

> Single, against innumberable hordes of tyrants and slaves, who menace her rising liberty, the French nation would have a right to reclaim the obligations imposed on the United States, by the treaties she has contracted with them, and which she has cemented with her blood; but strong in the greatness of her means, and of the power of her principles, not less redoubtable to her enemies than the victorious arm which she opposes to their rage, she comes, in the very time when the emissaries of our common enemies are making useless efforts to neutralize the gratitude—to damp the zeal—to weaken or cloud the view of your fellow-citizens; she comes, I say—that generous nation—that faithful friend—to labor still to increase the prosperity, and add to the happiness which she is pleased to see them enjoy.[1]

Genet's impassioned plea did nothing to modify Washington's previous decision that it was inadvisable to make new

1. To Jefferson, May 23, 1793, *American State Papers,* Walter Lowrie and Matthew St. Clair Clarke, eds., *Foreign Relations* (1832), I, 147. [Hereinafter cited as *ASPFR*.]

agreements with France until internal political conditions were stabilized. Since the French Minister seemed content with Jefferson's oral explanation that nothing could be done before Congress met, the matter rested and no formal reply was made. In any case both Genet and the Secretary of State were too preoccupied by immediate problems arising from the application of the President's proclamation to discuss treaty projects.

When Genet arrived in Philadelphia, Ternant presented him with Jefferson's formal protests concerning French privateering. The least important of these related to the *Grange*, a prize taken by the *Embuscade* in Delaware Bay. Jefferson also informed the French Minister that the United States was on a friendly footing with both belligerents and could not permit France to outfit privateers in American ports. To do so would be "to wage war on nations" with which the United States was at peace. Finally, the Secretary of State forbade the condemnation and sale of prizes by French consuls in American ports. This, Jefferson told Genet, was a violation of the sovereign rights of the United States—only American admiralty courts possessed this jurisdiction.[2]

Although Genet's reply of May 27 was moderately worded, it marked the beginning of the conflict over privateering which led to his recall. He agreed to release the *Grange*, but he raised basic questions concerning the application of the Treaty of Commerce of 1778. What, he asked was the purpose of the clause forbidding the enemies of France from equipping privateers or selling prizes in American ports, if this privilege were not to be granted to France? He could not see any possible ground for banning consular sale of prizes, for captured ships were French property and as such not subject to any other national authority. Why should there be any objection to arming vessels, when commissions were issued only to ships owned and manned by Frenchmen? True, there might be some American citizens among the crews, but this seemed inconsequential, since there were no laws prohibiting these enlistments.

2. Jefferson to Ternant, May 3, 15, 1793, Ford, *Jefferson,* VI, 236, 254–57.

In any case Americans entering French service "renounced the immediate protection of their country. . . ."

His note was free from the angry and embittered language of later protests, but there was not the slightest hint that he would accede to the rulings of the administration. He ended his letter with a little homily indicative of the future direction of his resistance:

> The French republicans, sir, know the duties which nations owe to one another; enlightened on the rights of man, they have just ideas of the general laws of society compromised under the common denomination of the *law of nations* (*droit des gens*) informed with respect to the interests of their country, they know how to distinguish its enemies and its friends; and you may assure the American Government, that . . . they will seize every occasion of showing to the sovereign people of the United States their respect for their laws, and their sincere desire to maintain with them the most perfect harmony.[3]

The President, unmoved by these arguments, instructed Jefferson to reaffirm his earlier statement. On June 5, in unmistakable terms the Secretary of State reiterated the ban on outfitting privateers and requested that ships previously equipped depart immediately from American ports. The Secretary of State avoided specific reference to Genet's comments on the interpretation of the treaty, preferring to defend the administration on the ground that it was the "*right* of every nation to prohibit acts of sovereignty from being exercised by any other nation within its limits, and the *duty* of a neutral nation to prohibit such as would injure one of the warring powers; that the granting of military commissions within the United States by any other authority than their own is an infringement of their sovereignty."[4]

Jefferson was not at all happy over the President's rigid interpretation of neutrality. He agreed that France should not be allowed to equip privateers, but contended that some allowance should be made for the fact that Genet had acted before

3. *ASPFR*, I, 149–50. Italics in original.
4. Ford, *Jefferson*, VI, 282–83.

he was aware of the President's rulings. There was, in the opinion of the Secretary of State, a certain logic in Genet's contention that the terms of the treaty implied that France had the right to equip privateers and sell prizes in American ports. However, he did consider Genet in error in his argument that the United States could not deny these privileges to France. Nothing in the treaty suggested such a restriction. From Jefferson's point of view, Genet's action in outfitting privateers was only a "slight offence." [5] In the cabinet, Jefferson had urged that the privateers equipped by Genet before he learned of administration policy should be permitted to use American ports and that their prizes should also be admitted. He succeeded in carrying only one point: the President agreed that prizes captured by the privateers outfitted by Genet before June 5 (the date precise orders were issued to the Minister) should not be restored to their owners as the British Minister was insisting.[6]

The French Minister considered the peremptory tone of Jefferson's note of June 5 highly objectionable. "I have seen with pain," he commenced his reply on June 8, "that . . . the President . . . persists in thinking that a nation at war had not the right of giving commissions of war to those of its vessels which may be in the ports of a neutral nation. . . ." The administration was adopting a position contrary to "the principles of natural right, to the usages of nations, to the connexions [*sic*] which unite us, and even to the President's proclamation." How could the President assume the terms of the treaty of 1778 were invalid "so long as the States, assembled in Congress, shall not have determined that this solemn engagement should not be performed . . . ?" Until Congress acted "no one has any right to shackle our operations . . . by hindering those of our marines, who may be in American ports, to take advantage of the commissions which the French government has charged me to give them." That the legislature would uphold his actions he never doubted, for the "fraternal voice"

5. *Anas,* May 20, 1793, *ibid.,* I, 229–30.
6. Jefferson to Hammond, June 5, 1793, *ibid.,* VI, 285–87.

of the people had been clearly raised in behalf of France. He made one slight concession: French consuls would be instructed to issue letters of marque only to ship captains pledging themselves to respect the authority of the United States and the "political opinions of their President, until the representatives of the sovereign [people] shall have confirmed or rejected them." [7] This ungraciously worded concession was quite meaningless. Not only did it ignore the basic issue that no commissions of any kind were to be granted, but Genet never bothered to transmit the necessary orders to the consuls. To stop the practice Jefferson was obliged to send a circular letter to the French consuls early in September informing them that their powers would be revoked if they continued to arm ships in American ports.[8]

The quarrel between Genet and the administtration over privateers was such an overriding concern that it thrust into the background lesser but equally irritating issues. In the absence of statutes or precedents, Washington and his advisers moved slowly, and at times uncertainly, in fixing the limits of neutrality. To a considerable extent, the administration acted on a day-to-day basis making decisions only as specific questions arose—a method in itself a cause of friction and confusion. One of the most immediate minor problems related to prize ships allegedly captured within American territorial limits. Since the three mile limit was not proclaimed officially until November, every case involving ships reportedly taken within American jursidiction had to be decided individually. Not only was this a slow and imprecise approach, but in the meantime there was no effective means of preventing the sale of contested prizes. It had been expected that federal courts would impound contested prizes, but they at first refused to assume jurisdiction. The only other alternative was to have ships seized by state or federal authority, a measure highly offensive to Genet, who

7. June 8, 1793, *ASPFR,* I, 151.

8. Charles S. Hyneman, *The First American Neutrality: A Study of the American Understanding of Netural Obligations During the Years 1792 to 1815,* University of Illinois Studies in the Social Sciences, XX (1934), 1–2, p. 95.

insisted that they were rightfully French property. The problem seemed to be solved late in June when the French Minister agreed that the consuls would hold up sales pending full investigation of contested prizes. He undoubtedly had no intention of executing this arrangement, for he was aware that the complete absence of adequate administrative machinery for enforcing neutrality meant that the consuls could do what they pleased. In any case he never issued orders to this effect to the consuls.[9]

Within two weeks after his reception Genet was not only disputing the ban on privateers and the sale of prizes, but he was equally outraged by another administration action. At the end of May two American citizens on the *Citizen Genet* were arrested in Philadelphia and bound over for trial on the charge of violating American neutrality by serving on a French armed vessel, and thus engaging in hostilities against a nation with which the United States was at peace. As soon as he heard of the arrests, the Minister dashed off a note on June 1 demanding to know what offense they could be charged with unless it be "the crime which my mind cannot conceive, and which my pen almost refuses to state . . . of serving France, and defending with her children the common and glorious cause of liberty." How was it possible that they could be arrested when there were no laws forbidding enlistment in the service of a foreign power?[10] He was right on this score, and his objection highlighted the difficulty of enforcing neutrality without specific statutes imposing punishments. Only one of the sailors, Gideon Henfield, was brought to trial in July before the federal Circuit Court in Philadelphia on the charge of conspiring to attack the property and citizens of nations at peace with the United States in violation of the law of nations, the Constitution, and the treaties and laws of the United States. Although the judges ruled that his offense was punishable by the laws of the United

9. Charles M. Thomas, *American Neutrality in 1793: A Study in Cabinet Government* (New York, 1931), 187–204.

10. To Jefferson, June 1, 1793, and Jefferson's reply of the same date, *ASPFR,* I, 151.

States, the absence of a statutory prohibition gave the jury (frankly sympathetic to Henfield) convenient grounds for acquittal. Genet, who had engaged Peter Duponceau, Jonathan D. Sergeant, and Jared Ingersoll to defend Henfield, was jubilant at what seemed another demonstration of the power of public opinion to frustrate administration policy. After his release, Henfield, who promptly reinlisted, was feted at a public dinner attended by the French Minister. Genet was so convinced of having bested the administration that he inserted a notice in the press inviting all "Friends of Liberty" to enter the service of France. Neither Genet's advertisement nor the acquittal of Henfield attracted many recruits. A reaffirmation of administration policy published by the Attorney General seems to have been an effective check.[11]

Still another rebuff followed on the heels of the June 5 ban on outfitting privateers. On June 11 Genet was informed that the President had rejected his request for full payment of the French debt before the due date. In view of the advances made to his predecessor Genet had been confident of a ready compliance. Moreover, he expected that his stated intention of using the funds to purchase grain and flour from American merchants would be an irresistible temptation.[12] The refusal was a serious setback for he had not been given funds to meet the expenses of his mission. The Girondins had taken it for granted that he could finance the expeditions against Louisiana and Florida from advances on the debt. The members of the cabinet, who had agreed with the President that it was unwise to settle the debt with a government whose future was uncertain, were unaware of the wisdom of their decision. Although it was not known in Philadelphia until the middle of July, the Girondins had fallen from power. On June 2 the National Convention, now dominated by the Jacobins, had ordered the

11. Hyneman, *First American Neutrality,* 130–31; Thomas, *American Neutrality, 1793,* 170–74.

12. Jefferson's letter and Genet's reply of June 14, 1793, *ASPFR,* I, 156; see also, Malone, *Jefferson,* III, 99; DeConde, *Entangling Alliance,* 211–12.

arrest of twenty-nine leading Girondin deputies and the remaining Girondin ministers (this included LeBrun) in the Executive Council.

While the President's advisers were unanimous in rejecting Genet's request, they differed as to the manner. Hamilton preferred a flat negative without explanation, a course Jefferson considered unnecessarily "dry and unpleasant." Accepting Jefferson's advice, Washington agreed to inform Genet that American public credit would be seriously injured if the government attempted to borrow the sum needed to liquidate the debt at once.[13] When Genet later appealed to the Secretary of the Treasury, Hamilton saw no reason to conceal his reasons for denying the request. He frankly told Genet that advance payment enabling France to purchase supplies was tantamount to assisting one of the parties in the war. Hamilton was so concerned about the attitude of Great Britain that he notified Hammond of the President's decision before Genet was informed.[14]

Never easily daunted, Genet replied to Jefferson's notification with a note denouncing the President's decision as implementing the "infernal system of the King of England, and of the other kings, his accomplices, to destroy by famine the French republicans and liberty. . . ." He announced that Washington's refusal to consult Congress left him no alternative but to issue assignments to merchants against future installments on the debt. When Jefferson expressed his disapproval of this method of anticipating payment, Genet sought a petty revenge by refusing to honor bills submitted by American merchants for supplies already shipped to Santo Domingo. Since advances for these expenditures had been made to Ternant, Genet was told that they would be honored by the Treasury and charged against the next installment of the debt if he refused to pay them. In spite of administration objections, Genet continued to issue bills of exchange against the installments due

13. Hamilton to George Hammond, June 10, 1793, F.O. 5, I: Genet to Jefferson, September 18, 1793, *ASPFR*, I, 174.

14. The pertinent documents are in Ford, *Jefferson*, VI, 302–15.

in 1793.[15] To Jefferson's surprise these were cleared by the Treasury. According to Genet they had been accepted because (in accordance with advice he had received from associates of the Secretary of the Treasury) he had negotiated his contracts with merchants known to be friendly to Hamilton. This story seems highly improbable, yet so deep was Jefferson's distrust of his colleague that he recorded it in the *Anas*.[16]

Genet's fury erupted on June 22 in a reply to a letter from Jefferson, who had justified the seizure by the Governor of New York of a ship armed by the French Consul. In the same letter, the Secretary of State had defended the detention of a French prize in Philadelphia pending an investigation of the legal ownership. For the first time Jefferson undertook to refute the interpretation Genet had placed on the Treaty of Commerce of 1778, citing Vattel and other writers on international law to prove that the arming of vessels by belligerents was incompatible with a policy of strict neutrality. "Discussions," Genet began, "are short when matters are taken upon their true principles. Let us explain ourselves as republicans. Let us not lower ourselves to the level of ancient politics by diplomatic subtleties. Let us be frank in our overtures, our declarations, as our two nations are in their affections. . . ." While Jefferson's argument was "extremely ingenious," it was inadmissible. "You oppose to my complaints, to my just reclamations, upon the footing of right, the private or public opinions of the President . . . and this aegis not appearing to you sufficient, you bring forward aphorisms of Vattel, to justify or excuse infractions committed on positive treaties." Was this an honest return for the generous commercial privileges France had recently granted Americans? Completely unyielding, he affirmed France's right to arm vessels as "incontestable" under the terms of the treaty.[17]

15. Quote is from Genet to Jefferson, June 14, 1793, *ASPFR,* I, 156–57. See also Keller, "Genet Mission," 212–19.

16. *Anas,* July 23, 1793, Ford, *Jefferson,* I, 246.

17. Jefferson to Genet, June 17 and Genet's reply June 22, 1793, *ASPFR,* I, 154–55.

Granted Hamilton's prejudice against France, his comment that this was the "most offensive paper perhaps that was ever offered by a foreign minister to a friendly power with which he resided" does not seem unjust. Genet's note was delivered shortly before Washington departed for Mount Vernon.[18] Jefferson told the President about it at a cabinet meeting on June 22, but apparently only described it in general terms. If Jefferson hoped to moderate Genet's defiant attitude and persuade him that he could not alter administration policy by appealing to public opinion, his powers of persuasion were unavailing. The Secretary of State was so discouraged that he confided to Monroe on June 28: "I do not augur well of the mode of conduct of the new French minister; I fear he will enlarge the circle of those disaffected to his country. I am doing everything in my power to moderate the impetuosity of his movements, and to destroy the dangerous opinion which has been excited in him that the people of the U.S. will disavow the acts of their government and that he has an appeal from the Executive to Congress, & from both to the people." [19]

If Jefferson had been able to read Genet's dispatches, his gloomiest apprehensions would have been fully confirmed. On June 19 the French Minister informed the Minister of Foreign Affairs that the administration was placing so many obstacles in his path that he had no alternative but to work secretly for an early session of Congress. Once the legislature met his success was certain, for public sentiment (in his opinion) would force a decision in his favor. This dispatch (only the fourth since his arrival) must have made puzzling reading, for he had not seen fit to forward copies of his correspondence with the Secretary of State. Not until October, much too late for the information to be of value, did he remedy this deficiency.[20]

For the moment the public at large remained ignorant of

18. Quoted in Malone, *Jefferson,* III, 114; Freeman, *Washington,* VII, 92.

19. Ford, *Jefferson,* VI, 323–24.

20. Genet to Minister of Foreign Affairs, June 19, October 7, 1793, Turner, *CFM,* II, 217, 254.

the conflict between the French Minister and the administration. Apart from the cabinet members and their closest friends, the only person in Philadelphia aware of Genet's behavior was the British Minister, for Hamilton kept him fully posted. It was with obvious pleasure that Hammond reported to his government early in July that Genet had lost the confidence of the President and was unlikely to regain it.[21]

From the very outset of his mission, Genet's intemperate language and intransigent attitudes damaged his case, leaving the President little choice but to order him peremptorily to observe American neutrality. In the light of his pretentious rhetoric and subsequent indiscretions it is easy to forget that Genet had excellent grounds for his protests. In the first place, there was solid logic behind his contention that the Treaty of Commerce implicitly permitted France certain rights by explicitly denying them to her enemies. If this were not the case, why had the treaty not forbidden these privileges to all powers? Moreover, as he pointed out, before France entered the war during the American Revolution she had allowed the United States the very same privileges now forbidden by the President. It seemed only appropriate that France receive the same benefits she had once accorded her ally. In addition, the policy of strict neutrality adopted by Washington ran counter to European practices.[22] Ordinarily European neutrals in wartime followed a course of friendly or benevolent neutrality granting their allies advantages denied other nations. From this point of view there were certain weaknesses in the American position, and it is significant that prior to his letter of June 17 Jefferson had not defended American policy by citing the provisions of the Treaty of Commerce or international law. Instead he had justified it as an exercise of the sovereign rights of the United States. Yet, as Jefferson reminded Genet, the mere fact that the Treaty denied these privileges to France's enemies did not deprive the United States of the right to issue orders banning them to all

21. Hammond to Grenville, July 7, 1793, F.O. 5, I.
22. Hyneman, *First American Neutrality*, 37–38.

nations. Nonetheless, as Hamilton had frankly admitted to Genet (and Jefferson probably found difficult to deny), American neutrality was in effect a pro-British neutrality. What Genet could not comprehend was that Washington had adopted this policy not out of animosity towards France but because he deemed it a practical necessity for the United States—as the only alternative to involvement in the war.

The Secretary of State was appalled by the hectoring tone of Genet's notes, for these pompous disquisitions about the sacred obligations of America to the cause of liberty merely solidified existing policy. He had hoped that Genet, guided by friendly advice, would state France's case in sober terms and obey the President's orders while waiting for new instructions from France. This procedure would prolong the discussion until the regular session of Congress, when, as Jefferson assured the Minister, American policy would be given a different direction. Genet could easily have drawn out the argument by referring to European precedents or citing writers on international law, but it seemed, as Jefferson observed to Madison in August, that the Minister had never read a book on the subject. Indeed, Genet prided himself on spurning the texts of these "jurisprudists" who represented the old diplomacy.[23]

Jefferson's efforts to induce Genet to moderate his position all failed. Nor was he successful in explaining to the Minister the exact relationship between the various branches of government. Genet could not be shaken from his belief that Congress occupied much the same position as the National Convention in France. In the Minister's opinion the President was merely the agent of a legislative body which was itself subject to popular control. On the basis of this analysis it is not surprising that Genet concluded that he must mobilize public opinion through a dramatic confrontation with the President. Even after he had been notified of his recall and when it was evident that Washington's policy had public approval, he persisted in this

23. Jefferson to Madison, August 3, 1793, Ford, *Jefferson,* VI, 362; quote is from Genet to Samuel Adams, October 28, 1793, cited in Thomas, *American Neutrality in 1793,* 169, fn. 3.

conviction. In September he was still explaining to Jefferson that "sovereignty in the United States resides essentially in the People, and its representation in Congress . . . [and] the Executive power is the only one which has been confided to the President. . . ."[24]

While it is apparent that Genet's imprudent and impulsive character as well as his persistent misunderstanding of American institutions were important elements affecting his determination to exploit public opinion to compel the administration to alter its policy, there were other equally significant factors which make his conduct seem less foolish. Unquestionably he was driven to act by the desperate situation in France: once again foreign armies were advancing, the rebellion in the Vendée was raging unchecked, food shortages and inflation were reaching critical proportions. Unless he could secure assistance from the United States the Revolution might be destroyed. He simply could not wait until December before obtaining a modification of American neutrality.

Everything that Genet had seen and heard since his arrival served to strengthen his determination to challenge the President's authority. Not only had the public reception convinced him that the people condemned the administration's policy, but he concluded that Jefferson would welcome a confrontation which would decisively defeat the Hamiltonians and ensure the republican interest a dominant position in the government. Genet assumed that Jefferson, whom he described as the "passive instrument" of the President, was totally opposed to Washington's measures. Undoubtedly, Jefferson in seeking to create a personal rapport with the Minister was partly responsible for this conclusion. Moreover, Jefferson never attempted to conceal the internal divisions within the administration. The Secretary of State, Genet later wrote, had "initiated me into mysteries which have inflamed my hatred against all who aspire to an absolute power. . . ." Thus, to his concern

24. Genet to Jefferson, September 18, 1793, *ASPFR*, I, 174.

about the plight of France, Genet added a quite undiplomatic commitment to the cause of liberty in America. In characteristic Girondin fashion, he believed it his duty to engineer the defeat of the party of aristocracy and place the forces of republicanism securely in power, and thus become the true instrument of the liberation of America.[25]

In concluding that Washington's proclamation lacked public support, Genet was influenced to a considerable degree by attacks on administration policy in the pro-republican press. At first the criticism had been muted, but as evidence mounted that neutrality was disadvantageous to France the attacks became more outspoken.[26] The bitterest assault—even Jefferson was taken aback by its harshness—appeared in June in the *National Gazette* under the signature "Veritas." The author remains unknown—he may have been Freneau—but Genet immediately concluded that the essays were the work of the Secretary of State. Jefferson, however, attributed them to William Irvine, a Treasury clerk, who (according to the Secretary of State) had been engaged by Hamilton to write pieces condemnatory of the administration in order to turn the President against the pro-French element.[27] In four numbers "Veritas" questioned the authority of the President to issue a proclamation of neutrality without consulting Congress.[28] The President, said "Veritas," had abandoned the nation's obligations to France, because he had accepted the frenzy of the "aristocratic few" and the cries of the "speculators, tories, and British emissaries" as the authentic voice of the people. In the last number, "Veritas" struck a then rare note, lashing out at the custom of idolizing one man to the extent of letting his opinions outweigh all others and thus stifle public discussion. By the time Hamil-

25. Genet to Minister of Foreign Affairs, October 7, 1793, Turner, *CFM,* II, 254.

26. "Varro," New York *Daily Advertiser,* May 1, 1793, and "Z," Richmond *Virginia Gazette,* May 22, 1793, are typical examples of this early restrained commentary.

27. Freeman, *Washington,* VII, 86; *Anas,* June 12, 1793, Ford, *Jefferson,* I, 235; Minnigerode, *Genet,* 181.

28. All four were reprinted in the Philadelphia *Dunlap's American Advertiser,* June 13, 1793.

ton began his powerful defense of administration policies under the signature of "Pacificus" (the first essay appeared in the *Gazette of the United States* on June 29), Genet was too committed to a defiant course to be turned back.[29]

Genet's opinions about American affairs were also influenced by his associations with extreme pro-French circles in Philadelphia. Shortly after his arrival he became an active member of the *Societé française des amis de la liberté et de l'egalité*, an organization of resident Frenchmen founded along the lines of the French political clubs. Here, from compatriots with only a superficial familiarity with American politics, Genet heard administration policies condemned and listened to gloomy predictions that monarchy would triumph unless the pro-British forces controlled by Hamilton were checked. He was exposed to a similar point of view during his frequent visits to the home of Dr. George Logan, a Philadelphia Quaker of advanced republican views. He also (according to the French Consul in New York) relied on the advice of obscure and unimportant refugees who made their way into the Minister's circle by flattering him and always agreeing with his prejudices.[30] Thus at the end of his first two months of residence in the United States, Genet's notions about America were no more accurate than when he left France. These errors were impelling him to take steps which were in essence directed at the overthrow of the Washington administration. He was no longer a diplomat, but a political missionary.

29. A total of seven numbers between June 29 and July 27.

30. Frances Sergeant Childs, *French Refugee Life in the United States, 1790–1800* (Baltimore, 1940), 166; Frederick B. Tolles, *George Logan of Philadelphia* (New York, 1933), 135–37; Hauterive MS Journal, October 30, 1793, New-York Historical Society.

7

Confrontation

WHEN GENET told the French Minister of Foreign Affairs on June 19 that he could only realize the objectives of his mission by rallying public opinion to defeat Washington's policies, he did not elaborate on his plans. Although he probably did not stage the precise issue which led to the confrontation with the President, there can be no doubt that he intended to continue outfitting privateers, confident that the people would support him if he were challenged. At the very moment in mid-June when he was so furiously contesting the administration's neutrality measures, he was equipping a privateer, the *Little Sarah,* in the port of Philadelphia. The *Little Sarah* (renamed *La Petite Democrate*) was a prize taken by the *Embuscade* and sent to Philadelphia to augment her armament from four to fourteen guns.[1] In view of the absence of any machinery for enforcing neutrality, it is scarcely surprising that the work on the *Petite Democrate* had been in progress for nearly a month at the seat of government before it attracted the notice of either state or federal officials. Jefferson received the first reports about the new armament from Governor Thomas Mifflin of Pennsylvania just a few days before the President was scheduled to leave for a two week visit to Mount Vernon. Before Washington departed on June 24, he instructed Knox to investigate the report, but the Secretary of War did nothing until July 5, when he took up the question with Hamilton and Jef-

1. For an extended account of the arming of the *Little Sarah* see Thomas, *American Neutrality in 1793,* 137–44.

ferson, who suggested that he write Governor Mifflin for additional information.[2]

Although Genet called on Jefferson later the same day, the Secretary of State said nothing about the *Petite Democrate,* preferring to wait until the charge had been confirmed. On this occasion Genet was in a fine mood, bubbling over with his plans about the expedition to free Louisiana from Spanish tyranny. Although he outlined some of the details of this project, he did not mention that he was equipping the *Petite Democrate* to support the operation against Louisiana.

The liberation of Louisiana, a favorite Girondin project, was the brain child of Brissot, who believed that Spanish authority could be easily overthrown.[3] Not only was the Spanish garrison small, but the reputed restlessness of the French inhabitants seemed to offer the prospect of an easy success. Brissot also counted on the cooperation of the Americans living in the West. In the published account of his American travels, Brissot had commented upon the determination of the Westerners to obtain the right to navigate the Mississippi by "good will or by force." "The slightest quarrel," he had written, "will be sufficient to throw them into a flame; and if ever the Americans shall march toward New Orleans, it will infallibly fall into their hands."[4] Girondin leaders assumed that American officials would not place any obstacles in the way of an operation from which the United States might benefit not only in terms of trade, but by the opportunity to acquire East and West Florida.

Girondin plans were seldom limited in scope. Characteristically, the dream of liberating Louisana was associated with the much grander vision of freeing all Spain's American colonies. Brissot had been so impressed by Francisco de Miranda, a Venezuelan revolutionary soliciting French assistance in

2. Freeman, *Washington,* VII, 92; *Anas,* July 5, 1793; Ford, *Jefferson,* I, 235.

3. For a full account of the Louisiana project see Frederick Jackson Turner, "The Origin of Genet's Projected Attack on Louisiana and the Floridas," *American Historical Review,* III (1897), 650–71.

4. Quoted in *ibid.,* III, 654.

freeing Spanish America, that after the European war ended he intended to underwrite Miranda's plans using Louisiana as a base. In the meantime Miranda was commissioned a general in the armies under Dumouriez's command.[5]

Fully cognizant of these projects before he left France, Genet was instructed to stimulate unrest in Louisiana and provided with blank commissions to use in recruiting expeditions against both Florida and Louisiana. In addition, he was expected to do something about Canada, either encouraging independence or annexation to the United States, but on this point his instructions were less specific. Joel Barlow and Gilbert Imlay, two Americans deeply involved in Western land speculations, assured French authorities that the Westerners would eagerly join in the movement to liberate Louisiana.[6]

Genet entrusted the Florida phase of the operation to Mangourit, the French Consul in Charleston, with whom Moultrie and other state officials cooperated. In spite of semi-official endorsement and much local interest, Mangourit's lack of funds rendered recruiting difficult and not until autumn did he succeed in raising a small force.

Genet did nothing about the much more important expedition against Louisiana until he reached Philadelphia, where he found a letter from George Rogers Clark offering to raise a force of 1,500 men to march against the Spanish garrison in New Orleans. This proposal, rather amazingly, had been made without direct knowledge of French interest in such an undertaking. Although Clark signed the letter, it had been drafted by his brother-in-law, James O'Fallon, an Irish born physician and onetime resident of Charleston. O'Fallon, a promoter with an incredibly complex involvement in Western land speculation, had hit upon this scheme as a means of augmenting his holdings. Clark (and it is O'Fallon holding the pen) asked in compensation only that France defray the cost of the expedition—he and his men would trust the generosity of that "great na-

5. *Ibid.*, III, 655.
6. *Ibid.*, III, 659–61.

tion" to reward them. Unaware that Clark had fallen on evil times, his lands held by creditors and his days befuddled with drink, Genet never questioned the glowing promises made by this once celebrated hero of the Revolution.[7]

The French Minister was unable to respond to this offer until late June when he engaged André Michaux as a confidential agent to bear instructions to Clark. Michaux was a distinguished botanist, who had lived in the United States for extended periods since 1786. His American connections and his friendship with leading Girondins made him seemingly an ideal choice. He was an honest and faithful agent, but, lacking Genet's revolutionary ardor, he was more interested in botanizing than in the liberation of Louisiana. It took him two months to reach Kentucky.

On July 5, just ten days before Michaux's departure for the West, Genet called on the Secretary of State. When the Minister had previously asked permission to appoint Michaux consul in Kentucky (without hinting that the botanist was involved in a special mission), Jefferson had refused, pointing out that the United States recognized consular offices only in coastal cities. However, Jefferson had obligingly provided Michaux with a letter of introduction to Governor Isaac Shelby of Kentucky. In this letter the Secretary had presented Michaux as a celebrated naturalist and now Genet had come to request that it be redrafted to indicate that the botanist enjoyed the confidence of the French Minister.

It was on this visit that Genet outlined his Western project to Jefferson, who considered the information sufficiently important to record in a memorandum:

> Mr. Genet called on me and read to me very rapidly instrns he had prepared for Michaud [*sic*] who is going to Kentucky, an address to the inhab. of Louisiana, & another to those of Canada. In these papers it appears that besides encourging those inhabitants

7. John Carl Parrish, "The Intrigues of Doctor James O'Fallon," *Mississipi Valley Historical Review,* XVII (1930), 230–63. It is not certain whether Genet learned of Clark's proposal before he left France. Thomas Paine wrote him about it on February 17, but the letter probably did not reach Genet before he sailed.

to insurrection, he speaks of two generals at Kentucky who have proposed to him to go & take N. Orleans if he will furnish the exp. about £3,000 sterl. He declines advancing it, but promises that sum ultimateley for their expenses, proposes that officers shall be commissd. by himself in Kentucky & Louisiana, that they shall rendezvous out *of the territories of the U.S.* suppose in Louisiana . . . and getting what Indns. they could, to undertake the expedn against N. Orleans, and then Louisiana to be established as an independant [*sic*] state. . . .

After listening to this account, which Genet offered him as "Mr. Jeff." and not as Secretary of State, Jefferson made a pointed comment: "I told him that his enticing officers & souldiers [*sic*] from Kentucky to go against Spain, was really putting a halter about their necks, for that they would assuredly be hung, if they commd. hostilities agt. a nation at peace with the U.S. That leaving out that article I did not care what insurrections should be excited in Louisiana." When Jefferson agreed to revise the letter to Shelby, the French Minister took his leave.[8]

As frequently happened Genet's account of this conference differed considerably from that of the Secretary of State. Writing to the Minister of Foreign Affairs three weeks later, Genet reported that Jefferson, who appreciated the value of the undertaking, had merely indicated that the United States could not participate in view of the negotiations about the navigation of the Mississippi in progress in Madrid. Nonetheless, Genet reported, Jefferson had made it clear that "a little spontaneous irruption" of the Kentuckians would not compromise the United States. Jefferson, he told his superiors, had also advised him about the best means of executing the project and promised to use his influence to ensure its success.[9] Obviously the Secretary's warning about involving American citizens had not made the slightest impression on the Minister. This distortion of Jefferson's comments (for the account left by Jefferson is un-

8. *Anas,* July 5, 1793, Ford, *Jefferson,* I, 236; instructions for Michaux are in "Correspondence of Clark and Genet," American Historical Association, *Annual Report for 1896,* I, 991–95. The separate instructions for Clark have not survived.

9. July 25, 1793, Turner, *CFM,* II, 221.

doubtedly accurate) was due to Genet's desire to impress his superiors with his achievements and to his habit of exaggeration. Yet at the same time he cannot be entirely blamed for his reading of Jefferson's observations.

Under the circumstances, a diplomat of a less impulsive temperament might well have concluded that the Secretary of State was only registering a formal disclaimer against the employment of American citizens while in fact condoning the undertaking. It was a low-key meeting, and it seems likely that Jefferson's warning was not delivered with the heavy stress given the ban on outfitting privateers. If Genet's project had succeeded in liberating Louisiana with the consequent benefits to the United States, would Washington have really hung the participating Kentuckians? The only advice Jefferson seems to have given Genet was to suggest that he confer with Senator John Brown of Kentucky, who gave the French Minister letters of introduction for Michaux. Brown, like most Westerners, was strongly anti-Spanish, but he did nothing to promote the attack on Louisiana. On the contrary, he wrote Benjamin Logan, whom Genet considered a likely prospect for a command, warning him that the administration would not condone hostilities against Spain while negotiations were under way in Madrid.[10]

Michaux left Philadelphia on July 15 accompanied by two Frenchmen (supposedly familiar with Louisiana) engaged by Genet as secret agents. Although Michaux had a generous supply of blank military commissions, the Minister's funds were so limited that he could only provide his emissary with the miserably inadequate sum of 3,000 livres (about $750). Genet assumed that Western enthusiasm would be sufficient to swell the ranks of Clark's army. Michaux was instructed to insert appropriate articles in the press and recruit friendly Indians for the descent on New Orleans. Making a leisurely journey, he did not deliver the Minister's letter to Clark until September

10. André Michaux, *Journal of Travels into Kentucky 1793–1796,* in Reuben Gold Thwaites, ed., *Early Western Travels,* III (Cleveland, Ohio, 1904), 39.

16, and reappeared in Philadelphia to report to Genet only in mid-December.[11] Characteristically, weeks before his emissary departed, Genet sent a dramatic announcement to the Foreign Minister: ". . . I am arming the Canadians to throw off the yoke of England; I am arming the Kentuckians, and I am preparing an expedition by sea to support the descent on New Orleans."[12] If fantasy were the stuff of diplomacy, then Genet would have been a magnificent success.

It was not until late on Saturday July sixth—the day after Jefferson's session with Genet—that Governor Mifflin reported that the *Petite Democrate* was not only armed but that she was ready to sail with a crew of 120 including some American citizens. A special messenger was sent to Jefferson's summer home just outside the city, but it was too late in the day for him to return to the capital before the following morning. Concerned that the *Petite Democrate* might depart before the Secretary of State could return and concerned about the repercussions of a direct defiance of presidential orders, Governor Mifflin, who was well disposed to the French cause, sent Alexander J. Dallas, the Pennsylvania Secretary of State, to ask Genet to detain the vessel, stressing the importance of holding the *Petite Democrate* in port until Washington (then en route to the capital from Mount Vernon) should reach the city. Having been on friendly terms with the Minister, Dallas was appalled as Genet in a "great passion" refused to hold the ship in port and proclaimed his intention of defending the rights of France by an "appeal from the President to the people."[13]

On Sunday, July 7, when Jefferson arrived in the city, he first conferred with Mifflin and Dallas before visiting the French Minister. The conference between the Secretary of State and Genet was a long and acrimonious session, doubly taxing for Jefferson who was far from well. When Jefferson asked that

11. *Ibid., passim.*

12. June 19, 1793, Turner, *CFM,* II, 217.

13. Jefferson's statement prepared for Washington, July 10, 1793, Ford, *Jefferson,* I, 237.

the ship be detained for a few days pending the President's return, Genet reacted angrily. "He took up the subject instantly in a very high tone," Jefferson reported to the President, "and went into an immense field of declamation and complaint. I found it necessary to let him go on, and in fact could do no otherwise; for the few efforts, which I made to take some part in the conversation were quite ineffectual." The Minister reviewed with interminable detail the arguments of his earlier protests. Jefferson finally broke in, as Genet, in a calmer tone, complained about the President's failure to summon Congress to determine the extent of American treaty obligations. When the Secretary explained that the interpretation of treaties was within the President's constitutional powers, the response was impertinent: "He [Genet] made me a bow, and said that indeed he would not make me his compliments on such a constitution, expressed the utmost astonishment at it, and seemed never before to have had such an idea." Since Genet appeared to "have come into perfect good humor and coolness," the Secretary "observed to him the impropriety of his conduct in persevering in measures contrary to the will of the government, and that too within its limits, wherein they unquestionably had the right to be obeyed." The French Minister had a right to protest, but once rulings were made he must obey the President's orders until he received additional instructions from France. Genet listened silently and Jefferson thought he had finally impressed him with the seriousness of the situation. Although Genet would not promise to detain the privateer, Jefferson accepted the Minister's statement that the *Petite Democrate,* which would shortly move to a new anchorage, was not yet ready to put to sea, as an implicit commitment to keep her in port until the President arrived. He based this conclusion on Genet's "look and gesture, which showed that he meant I should understand she would not be gone before that time." [14]

While Jefferson seemed to have temporarily calmed the

14. *Anas,* Jefferson, *ibid.,* I, 238–40.

Minister, he had no real hope that his arguments would have a lasting effect. That evening, he gave free reign to his distress in a letter to Madison, whose counsel he missed:

> Never in my opinion was so calamitous an appointment made, as that of the present Minister of F. here. Hot headed, all imagination, no judgment, passionate, disrespectful & even indecent towards the P. in his written as well as verbal communications, talking of appeals from him to Congress, from them to the people, urging the most unreasonable & groundless propositions, & in the most dictatorial style. . . . If ever it should be necessary to lay his communications before Congress or the public, they will excite universal indignation. He renders my position immensely difficult. He does me justice personally, and, giving him time to vent himself & then cool, I am on a footing to advise him freely, & he respects it, but he breaks out again on the very first occasion, so as to show that he is incapable of correcting himself. To complete our misfortune we have no channel of our own through which we can correct the irritating representations he may make.[15]

In this letter Jefferson expressed another concern—the wide circulation given to Hamilton's "Pacificus" essays, which, added to Genet's indiscretions, would surely destroy the influence of the pro-French element. "For God's sake, my dear Sir," he begged Madison, "take up your pen, select the most striking heresies and cut him to pieces in the face of the public." Madison, occupied with personal affairs in Virginia, did not immediately respond to Jefferson's urging. Not until a month later, when he comprehended the gravity of the crisis, did he undertake to refute Hamilton in a series of essays signed "Helvedius." By this time many of the details of Genet's conduct were known to the public and Madison thought it advisable to restrict his essays to the question of the constitutionality of the President's proclamation rather than explore the extent of American obligations to France.[16]

At noon, on July 8, Jefferson met Knox and Hamilton in Governor Mifflin's office in the State House to discuss his interview with Genet. The other secretaries did not share Jef-

15. July 7, 1793, *ibid.*, VI, 338–39.

16. The first number (there were five in all) appeared on August 24, 1793. Malone, *Jefferson*, III, 110–13.

ferson's confidence that the Minister's statement that the ship was not ready to sail was a sufficient basis for suspending further measures to detain her. Over Jefferson's objections, Knox and Hamilton decided to mount an artillery battery in a position to fire on the privateer if she attempted to drop down the river. Governor Mifflin, considerably more amenable to the views of the Secretary of State, agreed that it was unnecessary to call out the militia to hold the *Petite Democrate* by force. During the meeting a delegation of merchants appeared and urged military action to detain the ship. The merchants, placing little credence in Jefferson's assurances, agreed to raise $6,000 by subscription (it was assumed the legislature would reimburse the contributors) to construct additional harbor defenses.[17]

In interpreting a look and gesture of the French Minister as an implicit promise that the *Petite Democrate* would not sail before Washington's return, Jefferson was not deceiving himself. He knew that the privateer might put to sea before the President reached the capital, but he considered that the circumstances fully justified his decision not to press Genet on this point. Jefferson explained his unwillingness to approve forcible detention of the vessel in a long memorandum which he sent to the President on July 10. He had opposed the use of force because he was "morally certain" that the crew of the *Petite Democrate* would resist forcible detention with "bloody consequences." The use of force seemed especially risky since a large French fleet was daily expected at Philadelphia. If it arrived during or immediately after an engagement with the privateer, the conflict might easily be expanded. Moreover, it seemed to the Secretary of State that a decision involving an act of hostility against a foreign nation was one that only the President should make. Were his colleagues, he wondered, just as ready to fire on a British ship violating American neutrality before exploring all the avenues of redress? He did not disguise

17. *Ibid.*, III, 116–17; Cabinet Opinion on the "Little Sarah," July 8, 1793, Ford, *Jefferson,* VI, 339–40; Philadelphia *Dunlap's American Advertiser,* July 9, 10, 1793.

the fact that his preference for France and his animosity towards Great Britain had played a role in his decision. In view of all the injustices the United States had suffered from Great Britain since 1783, was it not possible to show some forebearance to France, the generous ally of the past? Nor would he willingly "gratify the combination of kings with the spectacle of the two only republics on earth destroying each other" and thereby letting it "be from our hands that the hopes of man receive their last stab." [18]

Hamilton also explained his position in a report to the President. In his opinion Genet's "gross outrage upon and undisguised contempt of the Government of the United States" called for strong measures to prevent further violations of neutrality. The administration, he warned, would be dangerously weakened if it did not act decisively for "nothing is so dangerous to a Government as to be wanting in self-confidence or self-respect." He thought it unlikely, in view of the Minister's defiant conduct, that France would have regarded the forcible detention of the *Petite Democrate* as a grave offense, but if "war is to be hazarded, 'tis certainly our duty to hazard it with that power, which by injury and insult forces us to choose between opposite hazards—rather than with those powers who do not place us in so disagreeable a dilemma." [19]

On July 9, before Knox had mounted the artillery battery, the *Petite Democrate* slipped down the river to Chester, anchoring in a favorable position to put to sea. Obviously the look and gesture of the French Minister had meant little. On the same day Genet informed the Secretary of State that the privateer would sail as soon as she was ready. He saw no reason to order her detention, since there had been no violation of American neutrality. As a prize of the *Embuscade,* she did not come under American jurisdiction, nor was it illegal for him to transfer cannon from one French ship to another. His conduct could not be challenged on any basis: "When treaties speak,

18. "Reasons for His Dissent," sent to Washington on July 11, Ford, *Jefferson,* VI, 340–44.

19. [July 8, 1793], Syrett, *Hamilton Papers,* XV 74–79.

the agents of nations have but to obey." To this impudent announcement, he added an equally insolent protest about the "revolting treatment" which the United States tolerated on the part of British naval vessels, which stopped and searched American merchant ships on the high seas. He asked to be "immediately" informed of measures taken by the administration to "cause our enemies to respect the flag of the United States." [20]

When Washington arrived in Philadelphia on the morning of July 11, a packet from Jefferson marked "instant attention" was waiting for him. In it he found Jefferson's summary of the July 7 conference with Genet and Genet's letter of July 9 announcing that the *Petite Democrate* would sail. In view of this critical situation Washington—unaware that the Secretary of State was prevented from coming to town by a raging fever—sent a messenger to summon his counselor. In rather irritable tones he asked what was to be done about the privateer now at Chester. Was Genet to be allowed to "set the acts of this Government at defiance *with impunity?* And then threaten the Executive with an appeal to the People? What must the World think of such conduct, and of the Government . . . submitting to it?" He invited Jefferson to breakfast the next day at 7:30, but in the meantime, in view of the gravity of the problem, he requested an immediate opinion.[21] Unable to leave home Jefferson sent a brief note covering copies of the report of the cabinet conference of July 8 and the statements he and Hamilton had drafted justifying their opinions. He had, he added, just received further assurances from Genet that the *Petite Democrate* would not sail before Washington's decision.[22]

On July 12, Jefferson was able to join Hamilton and Knox (the Attorney General was in Virginia) for the conference scheduled by the President. Now that the *Petite Democrate*

20. *ASPFR*, I, 163–64.

21. July 11, 1793, John C. Fitzpatrick, ed., *Writings of George Washington* (39 vols., Washington, D. C., 1931–41), XXXIII, 4, fn. 6. Italics are in the original.

22. This undated note is in Ford, *Jefferson*, VI, 340, fn. 1.

was at Chester out of reach of either militia or shore batteries, there was no point in considering what could be done to detain her forcibly. Jefferson had the impression that Washington wished she had been seized as Hamilton and Knox had recommended, although the President probably would not have given such orders himself. While the President's counselors agreed that the outfitting of privateers in American ports was an offense against the proclamation, Jefferson did not share his colleagues' opinion that it also forbade the transfer of armaments from one French ship to the other or the recruiting of French nations. If he could persuade the President to agree to these principles, then Genet's offense might be mitigated, for the Minister maintained that the cannon had all been removed from other French ships. Hamilton, who was anxious to seize this opportunity to discredit the French Minister, the pro-French faction, and the republican element all in one fell swoop, urged the President to announce publicly his intention of requesting Genet's recall. Knox, Hamilton's eager cohort, was ready to go one step further, suggesting that Genet be suspended at once. The Secretary of State recommended a moderate course which would avoid risking a rupture by permitting France to repudiate an imprudent agent on her own initiative. Why not, he suggested, send all the Minister's correspondence to Morris to be submitted to the French government with "friendly observations?" [23] The President said little as he listened to his counselors disagree. Although preferring decisive action, Washington appreciated the danger of provoking a rupture with France. Since it was apparent that the secretaries could not agree, the President (hoping that time would bring harmony) fell in with Jefferson's proposal that the administration ask the justices of the Supreme Court for an advisory opinion about the validity of the American principles of neutrality. This delay, for it was ten days before the judges assembled, merely postponed an unavoidable decision and did

23. *Anas* [July 13, 1793], *ibid.,* I, 243.

nothing to modify the opinions of the parties involved. The Minister remained intransigent, and the President's counselors were as divided as ever when the cabinet reassembled some ten days later.[24]

24. Freeman, *Washington,* VII, 103–05; Malone, *Jefferson,* III, 118–19.

8

Liberty Warring on Herself

AFTER THE CABINET agreement to consult the judges on the principles of neutrality, a calm descended on the administration. The bitter discussions over Genet's conduct gave way to temperate exchanges about Indian affairs and Dr. Thornton's plans for the Capitol at Washington. Nor did the questions to be proposed to the judges generate any rancor. The *Petite Democrate,* source of so much acrimony, vanished into the open sea without a single comment from the participants in the controversy or a notice in the press. Even the exact date of her departure (it was after July 14) remains undetermined. The British Minister, usually so prompt to complain about French violations of neutrality, did not bother to protest.[1]

During this ten-day lull the French Minister was very much in evidence bustling about in a frenzy of activity. The long expected French fleet had arrived in the Chesapeake, escorting a hundred small vessels bearing 10,000 refugees fleeing from the Negro rebellion in Santo Domingo. The fleet, badly in need of repairs and with near mutinous crews, departed to refit in New York, leaving those refugees who did not sail for France to the charity of the inhabitants of the coastal cities. Genet hailed the fleet as a deliverance—a means of executing a grand coup which would advance the cause of liberty and minimize the

1. Thomas, *American Neutrality in 1793,* 142; Freeman, *Washington,* VII, 104.

criticism he could expect at home as a result of his quarrel with the Washington administration. His thoughts were preoccupied with plans for a coordinated operation between the fleet and Clark's western army to liberate Louisiana.[2] For the moment, diplomacy took second place.

When Genet entered Jefferson's office on July 16, the Secretary of State took advantage of his caller's euphoric mood to suggest that Genet, if he would give up the "pickeroons which had been armed" in American ports, could earn goodwill for France far more valuable than the "trifling services" of these privateers. The response seemed to indicate a willingness to moderate his previous intransigence. "He immediately declared," Jefferson informed the President, "that having such a force [as the French fleet] in his hands he had abandoned every idea of a further armament in our ports, that these small objects were now beneath his notice & he had accordingly written the consuls to stop everything further of that kind: but that as to those which had been fitted out before, their honour would not permit them to give them up, but he wished an oblivion of everything which had passed, and that in future the measure so disagreeable to the government should not be pursued, tho' he thought it clearly justifiable by the treaty." Apparently Genet, who had not in fact written to the consuls, was trying to strike a bargain: if the privateers outfitted before June 5 were allowed to operate from American ports, he would not arm any vessels in the future. Jefferson could not agree to a position so far removed from Washington's views, and consequently, he could only remind the Minister of the right of the United States to construe its treaties. Genet might protest, but presidential orders must be obeyed.[3]

That same evening, Genet went to the extreme length of a direct appeal to the President. During a reception at the President's house, the French Minister, in spite of Washington's unconcealed reluctance, insisted on a private interview. The only

2. Childs, *French Refugee,* 13–15.

3. *Anas,* "Note Given to Presdt.," July 26, 1793, Ford, *Jefferson,* I, 248–49.

record of this conference is to be found in a letter written to Jefferson (but never sent) in 1797 when Genet was angry over remarks about his past conduct made by leading Republicans. By this time Genet was very much convinced that he had been betrayed by Jefferson, who had engineered his ruin for selfish political motives. Allowing for the distortion caused by his bitterness, the letter is of particular interest since it reveals the Minister's peculiar inability to distinguish between fantasy and reality. After the President seated him:

> . . . I spoke to him as a man desiring right sincerely; I assured him that I had received and not produced the movement which appeared to alarm the Government, and which I believed to be only the simultaneous effect of the honesty and integrity of the people; I swore to him . . . that my correspondence was indeed lively, but that if he would deign to put himeslf in my place and consider that by his proclamation of neutrality . . . he had annulled the most sacred treaties, taken from the French people, at the time when it had the greatest need of it in order to defend its colonies, an alliance which it looked upon as a possession dearly bought, he would agree that unless I were a traitor I could not act otherwise; but . . . I would show myself generous if he wanted to break the treaties concluded with Louis XVI at the feet of liberty in order to draw up a new pact which would contain only principles eternally true and bases drawn from nature.
>
> After which . . . I added with conviction that the Republic would emerge with glory from all its difficulties; that its armies . . . [would] force Europe to sue for peace on the terms which France herself would dictate, and that then she would not forget the United States. The President listened to everything and said to me simply that he did not read the gazettes and that it was of very slight importance to him whether his administration was talked about. We went out, he accompanied me as far as the stairs, took my hand and shook it.

Incredible as it may seem Genet interpreted the President's vague comments and formal courtesy as proof that he had convinced Washington of the rightness of his position. He believed that the President, who had been misled by reports filtered through the Secretary of State, now realized that the French Minister was an honest and sincere diplomat concerned only about the interests of France. The next day, according to his narrative: "I ran to see you [Jefferson] . . . , you blushed on learning that I had had a private interview and you were expressing your astonishment at it when the door opened: it was the President himself. I arose; I looked from one to the other of you to see if I might read in your eyes an invitation to remain for which I would have willingly given a part of my life; but a very imperative sign from you forced me to retire. I saw you again afterwards. I used every method to find out if the President had spoken to you of my efforts but you were impenetrable."[4] Three years after this interview Genet still believed that he had won over the President, but that the Secretary of State had checked him. Genet's delusions were never easily shaken!

The furor over the *Petite Democrate* did not in the least diminish Genet's standing in Philadelphia republican circles. On July 14, he sat with Governor Mifflin among the guests at a public dinner commemorating the fall of the Bastille. A week later he was happily discussing politics at Dr. Logan's country home, where no one felt it necessary to exercise restraint in criticizing the administration while the French Minister was present. Jefferson heard Genet, whose comments on American politics were welcomed, tell the company that "Colo. Hamilton had never in a single instance addressed a letter to him as the Minister of the *republic of France,* but always as the Minister of France."[5]

Not until July 23, after the secretaries had drafted the queries for the justices, did the President resume consideration of the issues posed by Genet's defiance. His conviction of the necessity for vigorous measures had been reinforced by Edmund Randolph, who had returned from Virginia with a report (to Jefferson's amazed disbelief) that the people fully supported the administration. According to the Attorney Gen-

4. July 4, 1797, in Minnigerode, *Genet,* 421. See comment on this letter in the bibliographical essay. That an interview did take place is confirmed by Jefferson; see fn. 3 above.

5. Quote is from *Anas,* July 21, 1793, Ford, *Jefferson,* I, 246 (italics in the original); Freeman, *Washington,* VII, 106, fn. 34.

eral the only opposition was of a personal character.[6] Consequently, Washington proposed to the cabinet that Morris be instructed to insist upon Genet's recall and that Genet's ministerial functions be immediately suspended. This approach, according to Jefferson, was supported by Hamilton in a "long speech exhorting the President to firmness." Knox, as might be expected, concurred, adding some stories inclined to increase the President's irritation toward the partisans of France. The Secretary of State said little at the meeting.[7] He did not doubt that Genet whose "conduct is indefensible by the most furious Jacobin" must go, but as he observed to Madison a few days earlier: "I only wish our countrymen may distinguish between him & his nation, & if the case should ever be laid before them, may not suffer their affection to the nation to be diminished. H., sensible of the advantage they may have got, is urging a full appeal by the Government to the people. Such an explosion would manifestly endanger a dissolution of the friendship between the two nations; & ought therefore to be deprecated by every friend to our liberty; & none but an enemy to it would wish to avail himself of the indiscretions of an individual to compromit [*sic*] two nations esteeming each other ardently. It will prove that the agents of the two people are either great bunglers or great rascals, when they cannot preserve that peace which is the universal wish of both." [8]

The only positive action taken by the cabinet at this session was to approve a reply to Genet's protest of July 9 about the "revolting treatment" of American ships by British naval commanders, who seized French property on American vessels in spite of the provision of the commercial Treaty of 1778 acknowledging the principle that "free ships make free goods." The discussion of an earlier letter of June 14 in which the Minister had protested a court order stopping the sale of a

6. Ammon, *Monroe*, 100; Madison to Jefferson, July 30, 1793, in James Madison, *Writings*, Gaillard Hunt, ed. (9 vols., New York, 1898-1903), VI, 139.

7. *Anas*, July 23, 1793, Ford, *Jefferson*, I, 247.

8. Jefferson to Madison, July 14, 1793, *ibid.*, VI, 348–49.

French prize ended inconclusively, largely because Knox insisted that the reply take Genet to task for his comments about the President's conduct.[9]

In responding to Genet's note of July 9, Jefferson contended that the principle "free ships make free goods" had never been observed by the European powers. Although the stipulation appeared in the Treaty of Commerce, it had been understood that it was a departure from accepted custom. Before it could be generally applicable treaties must be negotiated with other nations. In the case of Great Britain, a nation with which the United States did not have a commercial treaty, the administration accepted the rule that enemy goods on neutral ships were liable to seizure. As the Secretary of State reminded Genet, this really did little harm to France, since most goods bound for France were owned by neutrals, and these shipments (even on enemy vessels) were not subject to seizure.[10]

Thirty years later Jefferson recalled Genet's rude reply. As he told Edward Everett in 1823, it was only because of a "determined system of moderation" that the Minister had not been summarily shipped home.[11] On July 25 Genet restated his protest about the "scandal" of the "audacious piracy" practiced by the British. In view of the willingness of the United States to sacrifice the interests of her ally for profit, he could only conclude that the "thrust of riches" outweighed "honor in the political balance of America; all this management, all this humility, end in nothing; our enemies laugh at it; and the French . . . are punished for having believed the American nation had a flag. . . ." [12] This letter, composed with an eye to its effect when published, ended any possibility that Washington might stay his hand.

After the meeting of July 23, the question of Genet's recall

9. Thomas, *American Neutrality in 1793,* 102–03; Genet to Jefferson, June 14, July 9, 1793, *ASPFR,* I, 152, 154.

10. Jefferson to Genet, July 24, 1793, Ford, *Jefferson,* VI, 355–57.

11. February 24, 1823, in *The Writings of Thomas Jefferson,* A. A. Lipscomb and A. E. Bergh, eds. (20 vols., Washington, D. C., 1903), XV, 412.

12. July 25, 1793, *ASPFR,* I, 165.

was laid aside for a week in order to formulate rules governing the conduct of belligerents in American ports. This task devolved on the cabinet because the judges of the Supreme Court had declined to answer administration queries on the grounds that the Constitution did not authorize the court to render advisory opinions. The cabinet discussions over the neutrality rules were marked by the usual clashes between Hamilton and Jefferson, although on this occasion more over detail than principle. The rules (completed on August 3) reaffirmed the ban on the outfitting of privateers. The only exception was to allow nations with treaties permitting the right of repair to use American ports for refitting. One slight concession to France was the recognition of the right to recruit French nationals in American ports—a privilege denied her enemies. Hamilton achieved one notable victory: the President, who was convinced by the *Petite Democrate* affair that the states could not enforce American neutrality, agreed to vest future supervision in the collectors of the customs who would report to the Secretary of the Treasury. In a circular letter authorizing the collectors to inspect belligerent vessels as they entered and departed from port, Hamilton included some additional regulations approved by the cabinet. He transmitted one exception to the rule excluding privateers of the enemies of France: they might enter American ports to take on provisions needed to reach the nearest port of their sovereign. The collectors were also empowered to bar the privateers outfitted by Genet and a list of the names was attached to facilitate enforcement.[13]

While these deliberations were in progress, Jefferson presented his own private bombshell to Washington, announcing in a letter on July 31 his intention of resigning at the end of September.[14] Jefferson had long talked of retiring to private

13. The rules are printed in Ford, *Jefferson,* VI, 358–59, and Jefferson's notes on the discussions are in *ibid.,* I, 252–55. See DeConde, *Entangling Alliance,* 222–26; Thomas, *American Neutrality in 1793,* 152–59; Hyneman, *First American Neutrality,* 77–89; Hamilton to the Collectors, August 4, 1793, Syrett, *Hamilton Papers,* XV, 178–81.

14. Ford, *Jefferson,* VI, 360.

life, but the timing of his announcement makes it seem likely that he was using the threat of resignation to exert pressure on Washington to handle Genet's recall in a manner which would not be offensive to France. If Jefferson left the cabinet in the wake of a conflict over Franco-American policy, the dissensions in the administration would be publicly exposed, thus opening the way for sharper attacks on administration policy.

The day after Jefferson sent his letter, the President returned to the subject of Genet's recall with the cabinet. Hamilton and Knox still insisted that the request for recall be peremptory, accompanied by a public announcement of his suspension. Jefferson continued to argue the wisdom of permitting France to act voluntarily on the basis of the evidence in the Minister's correspondence. According to the Secretary of State, Hamilton defended his views with a "jury speech of ¾ of an hour as inflammatory & declamatory as if he had been speaking to a jury." To Jefferson's surprise and pleasure, Randolph relieved him of the onus of always opposing Hamilton, by supporting the moderate course advocated by the Secretary of State.

On the following day Hamilton opened the meeting with another long speech to which Jefferson replied with the warning that the suspension of the Minister would play directly into Genet's hands by making the conflict seem a personal quarrel with the President. The Secretary of State also challenged Hamilton's allegation that the emergence of Democratic Republican Societies modeled on French political clubs was proof of France's habit of interfering in the domestic politics of other nations. Up to this point of the discussion Jefferson felt that Washington was inclined to follow the course outlined by the Secretary of the Treasury, when Knox distracted the President's attention with a "foolish and incoherent speech" during which he read a recent satirical attack on the President predicting he would suffer the same fate as Louis XVI. Knox, aware how such criticism irritated the President, apparently intended only to arouse his anger at the pro-French advocates. The result, quite different from the expectations of the Secretary of War, so fascinated Jefferson that he recorded the scene in some detail:

> The Presdt. was much inflamed, got into one of those passions when he cannot command himself, ran on much on the personal abuse which had been bestowed on him, defied any man on earth to produce one single act of his since he had been in the govmt which has not been done on the purest motives, that . . . *by god* he had rather be in his grave than in his present situation. That he had rather be on his farm than to be made *emperor of the world* and yet they were charging him with wanting to be a King. That this *rascal Freneau* sent him 3 of his papers every day, . . . that he could see in this nothing but an impudent design to insult him.

After this outburst there was an embarrassed silence and the meeting broke up.[15]

Laboring under the strain of tedious cabinet meetings with quarrelsome secretaries in the oppressive summer heat, it is not surprising that Washington lost his temper. There is no doubt that he was both angry and personally hurt by the increasing tide of press criticism directed against his proclamation and against the failure of the administration to observe its treaty obligations to France. Accustomed to constant adulation as the hero of the struggle for independence, it was not easy for Washington to accept criticism of his public policy. As Jefferson commented in 1797, the President's "mind had so long been used to unlimited applause that it could not brook contradiction, or even advice offered unasked." [16]

Presidential policies had many advocates in the press but none was more effective than Hamilton. After completing "Pacificus," the Secretary of the Treasury took up his pen late in July as "No Jacobin" to defend the administration's interpretation of the Treaty of Commerce of 1778 and to refute Genet's contentions about American obligations to France.[17] The "No

15. *Anas,* August 1–2, 1793, *ibid.,* I, 252–54. Italics are in the original.

16. Jefferson to Archibald Stuart, January 4, 1797, quoted in DeConde, *Entangling Alliance,* 509.

17. They appeared between July 31 and August 28, 1793, and are reprinted in Syrett, *Hamilton Papers,* XV, 145–306, *passim.*

Jacobin" essays were ostensibly an answer to an article signed "Jacobin" published on July 13 in *Dunlap's American Daily Advertiser* defending Genet's right to outfit privateers. Charging that "Jacobin" was none other than the French Minister, Hamilton began a long analysis (nine numbers in all) of the American interpretation of neutrality by citing European usages and writers on international law.[18] In these essays Hamilton was as much concerned with destroying the French Minister by publicizing his conflict with the administration as with the defense of presidential policy. Although Washington had complained to Jefferson about attacks on the executive, he seemingly considered it quite proper for the Secretary of the Treasury to participate in the press debate and even, on occasion, make use of confidential information. Moreover, the President apparently did not realize that in condoning the activities of the Secretary of the Treasury, he was making himself a party to the partisan struggle, for Hamilton's articles were just as violent and extreme as those produced by administration critics. Hamilton opened the first "No Jacobin" with a bit of news not generally known to the public: "It has been publicly rumored in this City that the Minister of the French Republic *has threatened to appeal from the President to the People.*" [19] The fact of the matter is that Hamilton was undertaking precisely what he accused Genet of doing: using public opinion to influence administration policy. It was a bold step with repercussions far greater than the Secretary of the Treasury anticipated.

In a calmer mood when he met the cabinet on August 3, the President sought the advice of his department heads about Hammond's demand that the United States indemnify the owners of prizes captured by Genet's privateers. The secretaries quickly agreed that the French Minister be requested to re-

18. Hamilton attributed "Jacobin" (to which he was replying) to Genet on the ground that the phrases and wording had a French turn. Genet aparently wrote for the press, but none of his essays have been identified. Pascal, the Secretary of legation, also wrote for the press.

19. Syrett, *Hamilton Papers,* XV, 145. Italics in original.

store all prizes captured since June 5. If he failed to do so then the United States expected France to compensate the owners. Hamilton's suggestion that the privateers outfitted by Genet be forcibly seized if they attempted to enter American ports was rejected by the President, who agreed with the Secretary of State that it was an unnecessarily provocative policy. The President also canvassed the secretaries about the possibility of calling Congress into an early session—a proposal opposed by all except Jefferson. The Secretary of State, who had been unwilling earlier in the year to summon the old Congress, was prepared to take his chances with the newly elected body, which he assumed would be less subject to Hamiltonian influence. In Jefferson's opinion his colleagues did not want Congress to meet until Genet had been recalled, lest some action be taken to give American neutrality a pro-French inclination.[20]

Unfortunately Jefferson's record of the cabinet conferences relating to Genet's recall breaks off at this point, making it impossible to trace the interplay between the secretaries or to weigh the factors which induced Washington to follow the course recommended by the Secretary of State. Undoubtedly the President's decision was influenced by his desire to retain Jefferson in the cabinet until Genet had been recalled.

During the month which had elapsed since the crisis over the *Petite Democrate,* Washington and the cabinet had resolved most of the problems arising from the incident except for the central one—the manner of handling Genet's recall. Should it be a peremptory demand with immediate suspension of the Minister, as Hamilton wished, or should it be couched as a tactfully worded request enabling France to remove him as a friendly act, in accordance with Jefferson's preference? Whatever course was adopted Washington considered it essential

20. *Anas,* August 3, 1793, *Jefferson,* I, 254–55. On August 5 Jefferson informed Genet of the administration decision that France was expected to pay indemnities for ships seized before June 5; *ASPFR,* I, 167. The matter was handled in such a way that the United States did not commit itself to pay in the event that France refused. See Thomas, *American Neutrality in 1793,* 196–200.

that Jefferson remain in the cabinet until the crisis was resolved. It was with this necessity in mind that Washington rode out to Jefferson's country home on August 6 to plead with him to remain in office until the end of the Congressional session when Hamilton intended to retire. Washington began the interview by stressing the inconvenience of their leaving the government at different times. If they departed at the same time in the spring, it would be much easier for him to find replacements and balance geographical and other considerations in making appointments. Jefferson cited as his reasons for retiring both the need to look after his private affairs and his distaste for the political atmosphere of Philadelphia: "I expressed to him my excessive repugnance to public life, the particular uneasiness of my situation in this place where the laws of society oblige me always to move exactly in the circle which I know to bear me peculiar hatred, that is to say the wealthy aristocrats, the merchants connected closely with England, the new created paper fortunes; that thus surrounded, my words were caught, multiplied, misconstrued, & even fabricated & spread abroad to my injury. . . ." Further, he continued, "there was such an opposition of view between myself & another part of the admn as to render [my post] . . . peculiarly unpleasing, and to destroy the necessary harmony." Although he was not in contact with "what is called the Republican party" in Philadelphia, he assured Washington on the basis of his familiarity with members of that group in Congress, that they were not attempting to undermine the new government. During the next session the Republicans would attempt nothing except to render Congress independent of the executive. Nor would they precipitate a crisis over Genet, for once the extent of his misconduct was known "he would be abandoned. . . ."

Washington conceded that the motives of the "Republican party were perfectly pure," but "when men put a machine in motion it is impossible for them to stop it exactly where they would chuse. . . ." As the President voiced his opposition to monarchy and questioned whether such a party really existed, Jefferson interrupted him, saying "no rational man in the U.S.

suspects you of any other disposn, but there does not pass a week in which we cannot prove declns dropping from the monarchical part that our government is good for nothing, it is a milk & water thing which cannot support itself, we must knock it down & set up something of more energy." They then turned to the question of Jefferson's successor. By a lengthy process of reduction Washington eliminated one suggested candidate after another until it seemed that the choice would fall on a political mediocrity inexperienced in foreign affairs, and, by implication, leaving Hamilton in control of foreign policy. Not until five days later—by this time the President had decided in favor of Jefferson's method of requesting Genet's recall—did the Secretary of State agree to remain until the end of the year provided he could go to Virginia in the autumn to attend to his personal affairs.[21]

Much of Washington's apprehension that the republicans might attempt to destroy the government can be attributed to Hamilton's comments in private and in the cabinet that the recently organized Democratic Republican Societies constituted a threat to the security of the government. It was suggested that these clubs, like their French counterparts, would inevitably sponsor mob uprisings. If this was not their aim, why then the inflammatory resolves and manifestoes on behalf of France, liberty, and republicanism? While many, including the President, believed that Genet had a hand in establishing these Societies, there was no real basis for this conclusion. The first to be organized was the German American Republican Society formed by Peter Muhlenburg among the Pennsylvania Germans before Genet landed in Charleston. Shortly after his arrival a second club appeared in Norfolk, but it had no connection with the French Minister. Of the thirty-seven Democratic Societies which were established Genet can be associated with only two.

Shortly after he reached Philadelphia, David Rittenhouse, Charles Biddle, Peter S. Duponceau, George Logan, Alexander J. Dallas, and other leading citizens founded the Democratic

21. Jefferson, *Anas,* August 6, 1793, Ford, *Jefferson*, I, 256–59.

Society of Pennsylvania. Although Genet claimed to have suggested the name (the founders had wanted to call it the Sons of Liberty), he does not seem to have been an active participant in its affairs. The Philadelphia Society was not only the largest to be established (over 200 members), but it included some of the most distinguished leaders in the state. Most of the other organizations were composed of young men without significant political influence.[22]

Genet was most directly involved with the Philadelphia French Society of the Friends of Liberty composed of resident Frenchmen. He not only served as president, but helped draft the constitution which pledged the members to uphold governments dedicated to the preservation of the rights of man. Its most important activity was to maintain dossiers about Santo Domingan refugees, most of whom he (quite rightly) regarded as royalists for they blamed the island upheaval on the act of the Girondin-dominated Legislative Assembly granting citizenship to free mulattoes.

After the Jacobin seizure of power in 1793 and the Reign of Terror, fears mounted about the danger posed by these clubs. Washington, for example, was convinced that the Democratic Societies established by the "diabolical" Genet were responsible for the Whiskey Rebellion in 1794.[23] The President's denunciation of the Societies in his annual message of 1794, together with a better public understanding of their role in the French Revolution, led to their gradual decline in 1795.

Shortly before August 11—the day on which the Secretary of State informed the President of his intention to remain in office until the end of the year—Washington approved Jefferson's recommendation that the request for Genet's recall be made in a moderately worded letter to the American Minister in Paris. In order to avoid a rupture with France, the President agreed that the request should not be presented as a peremp-

22. Childs, *French Refugee,* 166–69; Minnigerode, *Jefferson,* 219–20. There are items in the Genet Papers, relating to the affairs of the club organized among resident French citizens.

23. October 8, 1794, Washington, *Writings,* XXXIV, 523.

tory demand, but rather to let the facts speak for themselves. Thus, when Morris showed the letter to the Committee of Public Safety, the recall would be made as an act of good will towards a friendly power. Jefferson completed his first draft of the dispatch to Morris on August 15 and then the cabinet reviewed it paragraph by paragraph on August 20.[24]

It was a long letter (it occupies twenty pages in Jefferson's printed writings), reviewing the Minister's conduct with damning citations from his correspondence. The case for recall was rested on his defiance of American neutrality and his refusal to accept the American interpretation of France's treaty rights while waiting for further instructions. Jefferson summed up the argument concisely in one brief passage: "When the government forbids their citizens to arm and engage in war, he undertakes to arm and engage them. When they forbid vessels to be fitted in their ports for cruising with the nations with whom they are at peace, he commissions them to fight and cruise. When they forbid an unceded jurisdiction to be exercised within their territory by foreign agents, he undertakes to uphold that exercise, and to avow it openly." In effect Genet had placed himself on the same footing as the government of the United States, behaving as if he were a "co-sovereign." Nothing was said of his threat to appeal to the people, nor of his plans to organize an expedition against Louisiana. The latter, of course, had not been a matter of conflict between the Minister and the administration.

Only one passage in Jefferson's letter created a difference of opinion in the cabinet. Since Jefferson wished to avoid offending France, he had stressed the point that Genet's activities tended to embroil the two nations and thereby "add still another nation to the enemies of his country & draw on both a reproach, which it is hoped will never stain the history of either, that of

24. *Anas,* August 20, 1793, Ford, *Jefferson,* I, 259–60; "Cabinet Opinion on Recall of Genet," August 23, 1793, *ibid.,* VI, 397; Malone, *Jefferson,* III, 125–28. The letter to Morris was not put in final form until August 23, but it is dated August 16, the date of the last document enclosed. It was sent to Morris by special messenger. It is printed in Ford, *Jefferson,* VI, 371–93.

liberty warring on herself." At Hamilton's insistence the italicized phrase was deleted. The Secretary of the Treasury considered it objectionable because it seemed to suggest that the cause of France was the cause of liberty, a position with which he could not agree. Although the President was willing to let the phrase stand, he yielded to the combined pressure of Hamilton, Knox, and Randolph, instructing Jefferson to delete it. The loss was not serious, for other phrases testifying to continued American friendship with France were allowed to stand. Jefferson not only carried the day as to the manner of requesting Genet's recall, but he also scored another victory over his antagonist: the President had not yielded to Hamilton's determined campaign to suspend Genet's functions.[25]

Although Jefferson felt that he had succeeded in preventing a rupture with France over the Genet affair, his triumph, as he was well aware, was only tactical. In terms of larger policy decisions, Hamilton remained the dominant influence in shaping American relations with the belligerent powers. The Secretary of the Treasury had managed to forge a pro-British neutrality, not by granting Britain special favors, for in fact Britain (well provided with harbors in Canada) did not need them, but by denying France privileges which that nation had expected to enjoy under the terms of the treaties of 1778. Yet Hamilton was by no means satisfied, for he had not achieved one of his major objectives—the destruction of the pro-French element. As long as the President refused to make public his decision to recall Genet and the circumstances behind it, the opponents of the administration could not be discredited. Determined not to let this golden opportunity slip by, Hamilton shifted the scene of combat from the cabinet to the public arena. At the very time that Jefferson was drafting the letter to Morris, the Secretary of the Treasury was setting the stage for a

25. *Anas,* August 20, 1793, Ford, *Jefferson,* I, 259–60. Italics are in the original. There was no public announcement of the decision to recall Genet and nothing was leaked to the press on this point. Hamilton, however, saw to it that Hammond was informed of the decision. See Hammond to Grenville, August 10, 1793, Great Britain, Public records Office, F.O. 5, I, Photostat in LC.

public exposé of the Minister's indiscretions, and particularly of Genet's threat to appeal to the people. In view of Washington's sacrosanct position, Hamilton never doubted that this last revelation was sufficient to destroy the friends of France. Hamilton's actions gave rise to a public controversy which radically affected the course of American political developments.

9

Adjutant General Edmond Genet

EARLY IN AUGUST, as Washington debated the fate of the French Minister with the cabinet, Genet, completely unaware that his recall was under consideration, departed for New York to plan the future operations of the fleet so unexpectedly placed at his disposal.[1] After his frustrations in Philadelphia he now believed he had within his grasp the means of realizing one of the prime objectives of his mission—the liberation of Canada and Louisiana. A success of this magnitude would be more than sufficient to deflect criticism away from his failure with the Washington administration. Moreover, as he confided to the Minister of Foreign Affairs, a French victory would inspire the American people, who seemed excessively timid, to join France in freeing the New World from the yoke of tyranny. As he contemplated the glorious prospect before him, squabbles over treaty rights, privateers, and prizes seemed inconsequential. Until the fleet sailed from New York on October 5, precedence was given to military and naval affairs. To give his orders the weight of authority Genet revived the title of Adjutant General which had been conferred upon him during his mission to Geneva.[2]

1. The size of the fleet at New York cannot be fixed with precision. In mid-September there were seven warships (two of them seventy-fours). They carried 290 guns and a complement of nearly 2,500 men. Before the fleet departed several smaller ships were added to the force. See lists of ships and crews in the Genet Papers, LC.

2. Genet to the Minister of Foreign Affairs, August 15, 1793, Turner, *CFM*, II, 240.

Before leaving Philadelphia, Genet indulged in a frenzy of dispatch writing to report on the status of his mission and to outline his plans for the fleet. As usual these communications were long on rhetoric and short on substance. References to his disagreement with the administration were too general to provide a meaningful guide to the status of his mission. One theme ran through these letters: public opinion would force the government to alter its policy. His dispatch of July 31 ended with the bombastic pledge: "My position, as you know, is difficult, but my courage fears nothing and I dare guarantee that I will achieve the goals you have set for me. My real political campaign will begin with the session of Congress, and it is only then that you will be able to judge your Agent." [3]

The Minister's unaccustomed activity was undoubtedly prompted by the news that the Girondins no longer held power in France. On June 2, after months of conflict, the Jacobins gained control of the Convention which ordered the expulsion of twenty-nine leading Girondin deputies. This news reached the United States in mid-July, but what Genet did not know at the time he wrote his dispatches was that early in July the Convention had ordered the arrest of the expelled deputies and also of Clavière, the Minister of Finances, and of Lebrun, the Minister of Foreign Affairs.

Genet had originally scheduled his journey to New York for late July, but postponed it when he learned that the *Embuscade* had put out to sea in response to a direct challenge from the captain of the British frigate *Boston*. In view of the public excitement over the impending duel—the engagement took place within sight of Sandy Hook—he felt that his reception would be all the more spectacular in the wake of a French victory, for he never doubted that the *Embuscade* would best the challenger. Not until he received news of the French victory on August 1 did he leave for New York, arriving on August 7.

Even without the added spur of the *Embuscade*'s triumph, Genet had every reason to expect an overwhelming demon-

3. Genet to Minister of Foreign Affairs, July 31, August 2, 1793, *ibid.*, II, 233–35.

stration in a city where Hamilton's most implacable enemies were men of power and influence. He could count on Governor George Clinton, Senator Aaron Burr, and the powerful Livingston clan to underwrite measures hostile to the aims of the Secretary of the Treasury, for political rivalries in New York, which were among the bitterest in the nation, had been intensified by the French Revolution.

Political contests in New York were all the more heated because of the power possessed by the Governor. Unlike his counterparts in other states, the Governor of New York had partial control over a considerable patronage and shared the veto power with a Council of Revision. Clinton, who had occupied the gubernatorial chair uninterruptedly since 1777, was a redoubtable politician with few scruples about using his official position to retain power. In 1792, he had shocked the Southern anti-Hamiltonians, who prided themselves on a gentlemanly decorum in politics, when he voided John Jay's election as his successor by disqualifying the votes of one county on a flimsy technicality.[4] Clinton had allied himself with the Southern critics of the Washington administration not so much because of a deep concern over national affairs, but rather because the rapprochement afforded him another weapon against his antagonists in New York.

Although Clinton's political convictions were solidly republican, he was hostile to the enlargement of central governmental power and had always opposed attempts to strengthen the Articles of Confederation. A great landowner with numerous tenants, Clinton prided himself on his republicanism, which did not imply either egalitarian or democratic principles. He lived simply, entertained but little (which earned him a reputation for parsimony) and was admired as a plain, honest man dedicated to the preservation of representative institutions and the protection of individual liberty. He was an open enthusiast for the cause of France, and gave Genet a genuinely friendly welcome, but he never advocated direct support for America's ally.

4. Harry Ammon, *James Monroe: The Quest for National Identity* (New York, 1971), 92.

In all probability he never reflected much about the extent of France's treaty rights. Like many others sympathetic to the plight of France he saw nothing incompatible between the treaties of 1778 and the President's proclamation which he enforced strictly, intervening forcibly on one occasion to prevent the French Consul from outfitting a privateer. Genet, always insensitive to the shades of American opinion about France, saw in Clinton's greeting another indication that popular opinion was not behind the policies of the administration.[5] Nor did Genet comprehend at this point that he was a pawn in the party struggle in New York.

The hostility between the pro-French and pro-British elements was more overt in New York than in any other city. The arrival of the *Embuscade* in June had set off a week of public celebrations. New Yorkers had eagerly greeted every prize ship sent in by the *Embuscade* as another happy proof of British humiliation and ultimate defeat. On July 4 the Tammany Society had feted the French Consul, who returned the compliment on Bastille day. Liberty caps appeared in all the taverns and failure to salute them led to instant unpleasantness. After the arrival of the fleet, street brawls between French sailors (abetted by local citizens) and British merchant seamen added to the tensions in the city.[6] The intensity of public feeling made New York the ideal stage for a public outburst of enthusiasm of the kind on which Genet placed far too much emphasis as a measure of the success of his mission.

On August 1, the New York politicos, informed of Genet's trip in advance, convoked a meeting of citizens to appoint a committee to draft a welcoming address. Ordinarily such assemblages were cut-and-dried affairs at which the citizens duly approved the plans of the local leaders.[7] This meeting, how-

5. Genet to Minister of Foreign Affairs, December 10, 1793, Turner, *CFM*, II, 278.

6. Alfred F. Young, *The Democratic Republicans of New York: The Origins, 1763–1797* (University of North Carolina, 1967), 465–67; Phineas Bond to Lord Grenville, June 8, 1793, *Annual Report of the American Historical Association for the Year 1897*, I, 529.

7. New York *Daily Advertiser*, August 7, 1793; Young *Democratic*

ever, did not go according to plan. Hamilton's supporters sought to disrupt the arrangements by circulating the report (leaked to them by the Secretary of the Treasury) that the French Minister had threatened to appeal to the people against the decisions of the President. Brockholst Livingston and James Nicholson, the principal organizers of the meeting, were taken by surprise when William Willcocks, one of their nominees for the drafting committee, endorsed a resolution for postponing action until the charges against Genet could be investigated. Willcocks's defection was particularly serious, for shortly after Genet's arrival he had addressed an open letter to the Minister, affirming his belief that American liberties were dependent upon the success of France and urging that America's ally be given all support consistent with neutrality.[8]

Willcocks's early enthusiasm for Genet had been shaken by the reports of the Minister's threat to appeal to the people. As he explained in two lengthy public letters, he could not stand idly by while a foreigner insulted the President. Revealing a sectional animus not uncommon at the time, Willcocks alleged that the French Minister was the "dupe of a party" composed of "certain designing, restless, and ambitious men to the southward"—men prepared to bring down the federal government and willing to incite insurrection, riot, and treason, if necessary.[9] According to Willcocks, these "dark, concealed, traitorous" individuals, who were using Genet to "raise their disappointed expectations, to repair their ruined fortunes," were the same men "who ride in their coaches, hold thousands in bondage, unable and unwilling to pay their British debts to the amount of a million sterling. . . ."[10] His suspicion that

---

Republicans, 475; Hauterive to Genet, August 2, 1793, *New-York Historical Quarterly,* XXXII (1949), 93; Rufus King to Alexander Hamilton, August 3, 1793, John C. Hamilton ed., *Works of Alexander Hamilton* (7 vols., New York, 1850–51), V, 572–73.

8. Willcocks to Genet, New York *Daily Advertiser,* June 9, July 12, 1793.

9. Willcocks to the editor, New York *Daily Advertiser,* August 6, 1793.

10. Same to same, *ibid.,* August 7, 1793.

Genet's friends were secretly working to destroy the federal government was not unusual, although the charge played but a secondary role in the public debate aroused by the revelation of Genet's threat. These letters illustrated what Jefferson had feared: moderate men with a deep attachment to the President would be so outraged by the Minister's conduct that they would damn his supporters as enemies of the government.

Willcocks's protest was insufficient to deflect the meeting from its purpose. As prearranged, a committee chaired by James Nicholson was appointed to draw up an address. The resultant document, which Genet termed the most vehement address he had yet received, was suitably flamboyant, hailing France for her "great and godlike work" in paving the way for the universal "triumph of Liberty." There was, however, one very slight note of caution indicating that the rumors about Genet had affected the committee's deliberations: "The voice of our government through its executive declared the neutrality of the United States. . . . We regard this sacred voice with attention . . . although in sentiment there is no neutrality." The Minister's reply, larded with phrases uttered on a dozen previous occasions, stressed the theme that the "cause of *France* is the cause of mankind, and no nation is more deeply interested than you in its success. Whatever fate awaits her, you are ultimately to share." [11]

The reception delighted Genet, restoring his *amour propre* which had been shaken by his difficulties in Philadelphia. He was met by the committee at Paulus Hook, ferried ceremoniously to the Battery, saluted by the artillery and escorted to his hotel (where the address was read) by an enthusiastic crowd assembled by the ringing of the church bells in the city. In reporting to his superiors about his welcome, he characteristically exaggerated its significance. The Anglophiles (he said) were enraged by the failure of their efforts to dampen the ardor of the citizens. So obsessed was Genet by the importance of these public ceremonies that he seriously believed the English Min-

11. Boston *Columbian Centinel,* August 17, 1793.

ister had gone to New York expressly to prevent a pro-French demonstration.[12] It never occurred to him that Hammond had been drawn to New York by the same circumstances as his French counterpart: the presence of a large French fleet. With the assistance of British Consul Phineas Bond, Hammond sent accurate reports home about the condition of the fleet and its probable destination. While he was aware that Genet planned further operations in American waters, Hammond was convinced that the demoralized state of the men left the officers no choice other than returning to France.[13]

In commenting on the future employment of the fleet, Hammond observed that Genet might use it to overawe the Washington administration, although he considered this rather unlikely. In view of the friction between the administration and the French Minister, it seems paradoxical that American officials never seemed apprehensive that Genet might use the fleet to coerce them into compliance with his demands. If there was concern on this point, it was never voiced.[14] In allowing the fleet to remain in port for such an extended period (more than three months), the President was generously interpreting the treaty provision, which permitted France to bring distressed warships into American ports for refitting. Yet what else could Washington do? If he ordered the vessels to depart and Genet refused to comply, the United States was incapable of expelling the fleet. When Hammond protested, Jefferson replied by pointing out that the treaty had not placed a time limit on refitting and that in this case the plight of the squadron was undeniable. Moreover, the Secretary of State did not think it damaging to Britain if the French navy were to lie idle from "year's end to year's end." In view of the ample naval facilities

12. Genet to Minister of Foreign Affairs, August 15, 1793, Turner, *CFM,* II, 240–41.

13. Hammond to Grenville, August 10, September 17, October 12, 1793, F.O. 5, I.

14. "Constant Reader," did raise this point in Philadelphia *Dunlap's American Advertiser,* August 21, 1793, but I have not located any other comments about the possible threat to the United States posed by the French fleet.

possessed by the British in Canada and the island colonies, there was little comfort for Hammond in Jefferson's explanation that this privilege was open to all nations and not an exclusive grant to France.[15]

After failing to disrupt the plans for Genet's reception, the Hamiltonians broadened their campaign to discredit the Minister and his supporters by publicizing his threat to appeal to the people. On August 6 (the day before he reached New York) the Chamber of Commerce adopted resolutions approving the President's proclamation and condemning attempts by foreign diplomats to communicate with the people other than through the executive branch. Much more telling was a letter appearing in the New York *Diary* on August 12 (and reprinted throughout the country) signed by Chief Justice John Jay and Senator Rufus King, who affirmed that Genet had indeed threatened an "appeal to the people from certain Decisions of the President. . . ."

In a dispatch on August 15, Genet branded the accusation false. Never had he threatened such an appeal, although in his opinion the feeble, pro-English Washington administration merited such an action. To establish his innocence he had just written a "very strong" letter to the President, which he would publish along with the reply and his correspondence with the Secretary of State. All this must have baffled French officials, for the tone of previous dispatches and all his talk about the ultimate effect of public opinion gave the impression that he did plan some kind of appeal. After all was not the promised publication of his correspondence a plea for popular support? Genet seemed to be denying what in fact he was actually doing —seeking popular backing to override Washington's policies.[16]

In his letter to the President, dashed off the moment he saw the Jay-King statement, Genet bluntly demanded that Washington deny "these dark calumnies" by publicly affirming that "I have never intimated to you an intention of appealing to the

15. Jefferson to Hammond, September 9, 1793, *ASPFR,* I, 176.
16. Turner, *CFM,* II, 238–41.

people." He also asked Washington to declare that the French Minister had never forgotten "what was due to your character or to the exalted reputation you had acquired by humbling a tyrant against whom you fought in the cause of liberty." Following the President's instructions, Jefferson (then in the midst of revising the letter to Morris requesting Genet's recall) replied curtly with a reminder that diplomats were not permitted to correspond directly with the Chief Executive, but must address all communications to the Secretary of State. "The President," Jefferson continued, "does not conceive it to be within the line of propriety or duty . . . to bear evidence against a declaration . . . whether made to him or others. . . ."[17] If Jefferson needed further proof that Genet would "*sink the republican* interest if they do *not abandon him,*" as he had written Madison a few days earlier, the evidence was now at hand.[18] There was, of course, an element of equivocation in Genet's letter. Jay and King had not accused him of having made the threat directly to the President. Even the well disposed considered his letter inadequate. As Robert Livingston noted, these charges would have a damaging effect on Genet's support in New York State, unless they were refuted.[19]

On the evening of the seventh, Governor Clinton entertained Genet at a reception attended by the leading anti-Hamiltonians, an occasion which had a momentous personal significance for the Minister. Here he met and fell passionately in love with the Governor's twenty-year-old daughter, Cornelia Tappan Clinton. The attraction was instantaneous and mutual. Cornelia, ardently republican and romantically attached to the French Revolution, was half in love with Genet before he ar-

17. Genet to Washington, August 13, 1793, Jefferson to Genet, August 16, 1793, printed in New York *Daily Advertiser,* August 22, 1793, and in Philadelphia *Gazette of the United States,* August 24, 1793.

18. Jefferson to Madison, August 3, 1793, Ford, *Jefferson,* VI, 361. Italicized passages are in cipher in the original.

19. Robert R. Livingston to Edward Livingston, Aug. 19, 1793, Livingston Papers, New-York Historical Society. Robert Livingston had apparently been shown Genet's letter of August 13 before it was published.

rived in New York. She envisaged him as a paragon of republican virtue, a dedicated patriot and defender of the rights of man, and her encounter with the attractive and witty Frenchman simply confirmed her infatuation. She made no secret of her emotions. The day after the reception when Delabigarre, one of Genet's friends, asked if he might tell the Minister that she looked forward to seeing him again, Cornelia, not the least abashed, replied affirmatively, and suggested that Delabigarre "mention all my love" as well.[20]

Although Cornelia's education had been conventional, she and her sisters had been allowed unusual freedom in talking about subjects regarded as a male preserve. In 1787 Abigail Adams Smith had been charmed by the fourteen-year-old Cornelia, who, she wrote her mother, was as "smart and sensible girl as I ever knew, and a high anti-Federalist."[21] Genet, too, was entranced by Cornelia's frankness and independence, so unlike the dull, convent-bred French *jeune fille* who was not expected to betray the slightest shred of intellect or interest in adult concerns until married.

Neither romantic attachments nor the mounting criticism evoked by the Jay-King letter deflected Genet from the main purpose of his journey to New York—the refitting and reorganization of the fleet for operations in American waters. The complex strategy which he envisaged was outlined in a letter to the Minister of Foreign Affairs on August 15. As soon as refitting was completed, he intended to divide the fleet into three squadrons. The first would be sent to destroy Halifax, recapture St. Pierre and Miquelon, and then support the Canadians who were ready to revolt as the result of the activities of his agents. The second would convoy merchant ships to France, while the third squadron would be sent to New Orleans (with a passing foray in the Bahamas) to support the Kentuckians, who, he assured his superiors, were waiting his signal to descend on Louisiana. Everything sounded not merely easy, but practically accomplished. All this was extremely vague. He made no seri-

20. Delabigarre to Genet, August 9, 1793, Genet Papers, LC.
21. Quoted in Roof, *Col. Smith and Lady,* 197.

ous effort to estimate the size of the British forces at Halifax or the strength of the Canadian garrison. As in all his projects there was a large element of fantasy. Were the Canadians really ready to revolt as he insisted? The only evidence he could cite was an inflammatory manifesto, which was never circulated widely. Were thousands of Kentuckians poised for an attack on Louisiana? On this score he had no information, for he had not as yet heard from Michaux, who was still on his way to Kentucky.[22]

Before these splendid projects could be launched, Genet had to refit the fleet, and, most importantly, restore discipline, for the sailors and marines were badly demoralized after the disaster which had overtaken them in Santo Domingo. Most of the ships in New York had been part of the escort of Thomas François Galbaud, the Governor General chosen by the Girondins to replace the special commissioners sent to Santo Domingo to restore order after the black uprising of 1791. As a result of this revolt (the first of many during the next few years) white planters had been expelled from a large portion of the island. Many had fled to the United States, which had advanced money to Ternant for their relief and also for the purchase of supplies for French forces in the colony. To prevent further disorders the commissioners had carried out the decree of the Legislative Assembly granting citizenship to mulattoes and free Negroes, a move detested by the whites, who became openly hostile to the commissioners. When Galbaud arrived at Cap Français (the only port still controlled by the French) the commissioners refused to acknowledge his authority. The whites, however, welcomed him (his wife was an island heiress) and pledged their support. In June, Galbaud, backed by the naval commanders and the whites, attempted to assert his authority by a military coup. At first he was successful, but, when the commissioners assembled black and mulatto

22. Turner, *CFM,* II, 238–40. St. Pierre and Miquelon, which had been retained by France in the Peace of Paris of 1763, had recently been seized by the British. Genet had sent an agent to Canada with the manifesto, Woodfin, "Genet," 430–31.

troops with free license to plunder the city, he was driven back to his ships and the panic-stricken residents sought refuge aboard merchant vessels in the harbor. As the city burned (it was totally destroyed and never rebuilt), the fleet convoyed the refugees to the safety of the nearest American ports. This terrifying catastrophe—the destruction of Cap Français involved a fearful slaughter—demoralized the crews who did not know whether to blame their commanders, Jacobin commissioners, royalists, or Galbaud, whom the commissioners proclaimed a counter-revolutionary. Temporarily Galbaud and his family were placed under arrest on the *Jupiter*, the seventy-four gun flagship of Vice Admiral Cambis who shared the command of the fleet with Vice Admiral Sercey.

Shortly after the flotilla arrived at Baltimore, Genet, Sercey, and Cambis agreed to send Galbaud back to France on one of the smaller ships, retaining the others for operations in American waters. Technically Genet had no authority over the fleet, but the commanders, whether they approved of his plans or not, had little choice. Without the Minister's cooperation they could not undertake the repairs needed to make the ships seaworthy. Moreover, in view of the confused reports emanating from France, which left some doubt whether the Jacobins would be able to dominate the Convention after the expulsion of the Girondins, the commanders were probably willing to let Genet assume responsibility for decisions which might not be approved at home. The Minister's intervention was doubly welcome since it was by no means certain that the officers could prevent the general discontent among the men from erupting into open mutiny. This danger was all the greater when the crew members learned that the fleet was scheduled to operate in American waters. The authority of the commanders was directly challenged by the refusal of the *Jupiter*'s crew to permit Genet to remove Galbaud to another ship. The men looked upon the Governor General not as a criminal to be tried in France but rather as a hostage guaranteeing their immediate return home. Galbaud encouraged the crew to resist, for he much preferred arriving in France with the officers who shared responsibility for the defeat at Cap Français.[23]

In solving the problems facing him in New York, Genet worked on the assumption that the Jacobins would consolidate their control in France. Consequently, in reporting to the Minister of Foreign Affairs about the condition of the fleet, he sided with the Santo Domingan commissioners in blaming the disaster on the "traitor" Galbaud. Even though he considered the officers and men loyal and patriotic citizens, still he did not think the fleet could be sent back to the colony without risking a mutiny. The men, he reported, were perfectly calm and sensible as long as no one spoke to them about "St. Domingue, commissioners, mulattoes, or Negroes." Moreover, since the black revolution had to be completed on the island if France wished to retain her colony, he could see no point in sending the fleet to Santo Domingo.[24]

Genet set about refitting the ships and restoring morale energetically and efficiently. Although as a diplomat his conduct seems to justify Gouverneur Morris' conclusion that he was a busy man rather than a man of business, his handling of the situation in New York partially belies this judgment. When faced with concrete organizational problems Genet did get things done and he did them well. On the managerial level the poor judgment and misconceptions, which marred his relations with the Washington administration and also prevented him from sensing the opposition within the fleet to continued operations in America, were not a handicap. Forming a war council with Cambis and Sercey, Genet, as an Adjutant General of France, ordered crew members reassigned throughout the fleet. He inaugurated a regular indoctrination program, instructing commanders to hold daily musters at which patriotic addresses were to be delivered along with readings from the Declaration

23. On events in Santo Domingo see Keller, "Genet Mission," 332–36; Childs, *French Refugee,* 13–15; and C. L. R. James, *The Black Jacobins,* 2nd ed. (New York, 1963), 121–28.

24. To Minister of Foreign Affairs, August 15, 1793, Turner, *CFM,* II, 238–39.

of the Rights of Man and the recently adopted constitution. To ensure the republicanization of the men he ordered the singing of patriotic songs, including the "Marseillaise" for which he composed additional verses. Genet himself attended these assemblies using the force of his presence and his impassioned oratory to remind the men of their duty to France and to the Revolution. Vacancies in the crews were filled with recruits from the ranks of the near destitute refugees, while contracts for supplies (including, as Hammond noted, winter uniforms) were negotiated with James Nicholson and other New York merchants. Genet disbursed at least $100,000 for refitting.[25]

He quickly restored discipline on all the ships except the *Jupiter,* whose men stubbornly refused to release Galbaud or accept transfers. They responded to Genet's pressure with a manifesto demanding that the fleet be sent directly to France and denouncing the secret war council as a device more suited to a monarchy than to a republic.[26] At the end of August, Genet resorted to strong measures. After unsuccessfully applying to the Mayor of New York for a warrant to arrest the ringleaders on board the *Jupiter* on the grounds that they had collected two pounds of arsenic to poison those refusing to join the mutiny, he issued a proclamation offering a discharge with full pay to all who wished to leave the service. If they refused to leave the ship, he threatened to occupy it forcibly.[27] Unable to obtain support on other ships, the sailors on the *Jupiter* abandoned the struggle. With the help of the crew Galbaud escaped on August 29 and fled to Canada, eluding Genet's agents, who tried to capture him. The crew then disembarked. Most accepted transfers but a hundred took the road to Philadelphia hoping to join Galbaud, for it was widely believed he had

25. Hammond to Grenville, September 17, 1793, F.O. 5, I. There is much information on the affairs of the fleet in the Genet Papers, LC. See also Didier, "Genet," *Revue des questions historiques,* XCII (1912), 82–84. To pay for refitting Genet issued bills of credit against future installments on the debt owed France.

26. New York *Daily Advertiser,* August 21, 1793.

27. *Ibid.,* September 4, 1793; Genet to the Mayor of New York, August 27, 1793, Genet Papers, New York Public Library; same to same, August 30, 1793, Varick Papers, New-York Historical Society.

sought refuge with the French colony at Chester. Even the Francophiles were alarmed at the movement of this armed band. Consequently, when the French Consul at Philadelphia requested their arrest as deserters under the terms of the consular treaty with France, Governor Mifflin readily called out the militia. The leaderless men were seized outside the city and imprisoned until the Consul arranged their release.[28]

The resistance broken, Genet entrusted the *Jupiter* to Captain Bompard of the *Embuscade.* A month later, on October 5, the squadron put out to sea. Among the vessels clearing the harbor was the *Petite Democrate,* now renamed *Cornelia.* The fleet commanders did not carry out Genet's orders to seek new laurels in Canada. Shortly after sailing the officers were again confronted by mutinous crews. Under these circumstances the commanders agreed to set sail for France rather than risk winter operations in northern waters without a suitable base.[29]

When the squadron sailed not everyone shared Genet's certainty that the liberation of Canada and Louisiana was at hand. George Hammond, who seems to have had more reliable informants than the Adjutant General, reported to Lord Grenville that the commanders would undoubtedly set sail for France in spite of plans for continued American operations.[30] Nor was the French Consul in New York, Alexander Lanoutte, Comte d'Hauterive, as sanguine as Genet. Hauterive, originally appointed under the constitutional monarchy, had worked closely with Genet during the refitting. Welcoming Genet as a hero of the Revolution, Hauterive had been charmed by the Minister's wit and impressed by his competence in dealing with the problems of the fleet. As the months passed, however, the Consul began to question his colleague's judgment. As he listened to Genet discourse by the hour about the forces mustered in Kentucky or the ease with which a frigate could capture St. Augus-

28. Keller, "Genet Mision," 347–49; Dupont (Consul at Philadelphia) to Genet, September 2, 3, 1793, Genet Papers, LC; New York *Daily Advertiser,* September 2, 1793.

29. Woodfin, "Genet," 617.

30. Keller, "Genet Mission," 354; Hammond to Grenville, October 22, November 10, 1793, F.O. 5, I.

tine, he gradually realized that all these projects were but a "chimera" spun out of the Minister's fancy. Genet, he recorded in his journal, saw only surfaces and seemed incapable of weighing the consequences of his actions. In view of the Minister's lack of judgment, the Consul considered it disastrous that Genet should surround himself with fools—men who gained his confidence by flattery and by always agreeing with him. Much as he sympathized with Genet, for Hauterive considered the American government fundamentally hostile to France, the Consul was shocked at Genet's imperviousness to suggestions not in harmony with his preconceptions. Hauterive felt that the defects in Genet's character made him unsuited for such a sensitive post in spite of the Minister's real abilities.[31]

Once the fleet departed there was nothing to detain Genet, but he remained in New York until December. Much as he was delighted to be near Cornelia (his "chère Republicaine" whom he hoped to marry), he was not held back by romantic reasons.[32] The outbreak of a major epidemic of yellow fever in Philadelphia made it impossible for him to return to the capital. Governmental operations were brought nearly to a standstill and there was almost no communication with Philadelphia. All persons coming from the plague infected city were quarantined—even Alexander Hamilton was not allowed to enter New York until five physicians had certified that he was in good health.

During August and September, Genet gave little attention to diplomacy. He did not write the Secretary of State until he had been in New York for a month and then only about a matter with little relevance to his mission. On September 6 he sent a frantic letter to the Secretary of State: "I have just discovered the most horrible conspiracy which has been formed against

31. Hauterive MS Journal, October 29, 30, November 2, 1793, in New-York Historical Society.

32. He used this phrase in a letter to Cornelia, December 23, 1793, Genet Papers in *ibid.*

the arms of the French republic; I have just discovered the whole clue and the proofs of the infernal plot which for these two months detained the French squadron in a state of nullity. . . ." His accusation: Galbaud (reportedly hiding near Philadelphia) and other traitors were plotting to join the English fleet in an expedition against Santo Domingo. According to Genet, refugees, under the pretense of returning to France, were chartering ships in American ports for an assault on the island. He demanded Galbaud's arrest and the detention of ships engaged by the refugees. Of all this he offered not a shred of proof.

Jefferson was not impressed by this portentous news, for it was obvious that the Minister only wanted to discredit Galbaud. He told Genet that Galbaud could not be arrested by American officials for offenses committed against the laws of France. If Genet provided evidence that the refugees were arming vessels to attack possessions of France, then the United States would act promptly to prevent their departure.[33]

When Jefferson received this letter, he was much more concerned over Genet's failure to fulfill pledges made earlier in the year than by this improbable conspiracy. By the end of August it was apparent that Genet had done nothing about restoring prizes captured after June 5 by privateers which he had commissioned. Nor were French consuls (as he had promised) impounding contested prizes until the legality of the seizures could be determined. Moreover, the consuls were still commissioning armed vessels in spite of Genet's assurances that he would instruct them to observe administration regulations. Consequently, on September 7 Jefferson sent a circular letter to the consuls ordering them to adhere to the rules formulated concerning the sale of prizes. The consuls were also forbidden to outfit privateers or to recruit American citizens for French ser-

33. Genet to Jefferson, September 6, 1793, and Jefferson's reply, September 12, 1793, *ASPFR,* I, 177. Galbaud was actually in Canada, where the British, fearing he had come to revolutionize the province, denied him asylum. He returned to the United States, remaining in hiding until the spring of 1794 when he returned to France. Keller, "Genet Mission," 359–62.

vice.[34] Genet responded vehemently on September 14. Why, he asked, should he be expected to issue consular instructions contrary to France's treaty rights? If his conduct had displeased either the "Anglophobists or Anglomen," he at least had "the satisfaction of having rendered an important service to my country. . . ."[35]

Not until a few days after writing this angry letter did Genet learn that his recall had been requested, for Jefferson had not forwarded a copy of the letter to Morris until September 15, a week after the President left for Mount Vernon.[36] The news was truly a shock. Although newspaper essayists had been discussing the French Minister's conduct for nearly two months, none had given the slightest hint that his recall was under consideration. His response was an enraged polemic—a "veritable logomachie" in Hauterive's opinion.[37] It was a letter written not so much to justify his conduct or refute the charges but with an eye to the effect it would have on public opinion when published in America and in France. It was an absurd farrago which began with a lecture on the correct interpretation of the federal constitution:

> Persuaded that the sovereignty of the United States resides essentially in the People and its representatives in Congress; persuaded that the Executive power is the only one which has been confided to the President of the United States; persuaded that this magistrate has not the right to decide questions . . . [which] the Constitution reserves particularly to Congress; persuaded that he has not the power to bend existing treaties to circumstances . . . ; persuaded that the league formed by the tyrants to annihilate republican principles founded on the rights of man, will be the object of the most serious deliberations of Congress; I had deferred in the sole view of maintaining good harmony between the free people of America and France, communicating to my Government, before

34. Jefferson to the Consuls, September 7, 1793, Jefferson to Genet, September 9, 1793, *ASPFR,* I, 175.

35. Genet to Jefferson, September 14, 1793, *ibid.,* I, 184.

36. There is no explication for this delay. Possibly Jefferson expected Genet to return to Philadelphia. See DeConde, *Entangling Alliance,* 300. Genet's response of September 18 is in *ASPFR,* I, 172–74

37. Hauterive MS Journal, October 20, 1793, New-York Historical Society.

> the epoch at which the Representatives of the People were to assemble, the original correspondence which has taken place . . . between you and myself. . . .

On he rampaged, branding the charges against him as calumnies invented by the enemies of democracy. Jefferson, too, must bear some of the blame. Genet accused the Secretary of State of betraying him after "having made me believe that you were my friend, after having initiated me into the mysteries which have inflamed my hatred against all those who aspire to absolute power. . . ." Yet, in spite of the deception practiced by men whom he regarded as friends, he still did not doubt that justice would be done to him when Congress investigated the conduct of the executive. Only the representatives of the people, he insisted, had the right to bring charges against the Minister of the people of France. He could not be dismissed by a single individual, for only a "despot singly may permit himself to demand from another despot the recall of a representative. . . ." For the first time in his official correspondence he complained about the behavior of Gouverneur Morris. Although he had touched on this matter shortly after his arrival during a private conversation at Jefferson's summer home, the Secretary of State had not attached much importance to these complaints, since they had not been followed by a formal protest.

Genet also took the opportunity to complain about the chilly reception accorded him by the "first magistrate of a free people," who had seen fit to display portrait medallions of "Capet and his family." He followed this with some bitter comments about the President's refusal to summon Congress and thus ascertain the "true sentiment of the people" in spite of Genet's "respectful intimation" that he do so. To let the world know the true facts, he proclaimed his intention of publishing his correspondence with the administration.

The scope of Genet's delusions seems incredible. Six months after his arrival in the United States he still did not comprehend the role of the executive in the federal structure or realize that the nation's devotion to Washington doomed all attacks on the hero of the Revolution. Although there was no reason to assume that the newly elected Congress would condemn administration measures, he believed (or so he asserted) that public opinion would force a reversal of administration foreign policy. His faith in popular demonstrations and in the effusions of pro-French polemicists as proper expressions of the will of the people was apparently unshaken. It completely escaped him that these activities were to a large degree tactical maneuvers in the rising party warfare and that he had become a pawn in the struggle to control the government. All the counsel and advice he had received from Jefferson and American leaders had not had the slightest effect on his opinions.

If Washington had seen Genet's letter in September, he would assuredly have suspended the Minister, but it did no reach Philadelphia until after both the President and the Secretary of State had left for Virginia. It was placed in a packe addressed to Jefferson, but it was never posted. The epidemic was then nearing its peak and governmental offices were completely disrupted. Consequently, Jefferson never saw Genet's letter until he returned to the capital in December.[38] By tha time there seemed no point in exacerbating Franco-American relations by suspending the Minister, since his recall was momentarily expected. The fact that Jefferson never replied did not disturb Genet, who, after all, had composed the letter fo public consumption.

The same bravado and assurance of ultimate success exhibited in the letter to Jefferson of September 18 was eviden in his dispatches to the Foreign Minister. For the first time sinc his arrival Genet provided detailed reports about events in America and supplied copies of his correspondence with th administration.[39]

In spite of his official blustering, Genet was privately les confident. He knew that the French government would prob

38. See note in *ASPFR,* I, 174. The Chief Clerk of the Stat Department had fled the city with his family, Malone, *Jefferson,* III, 14
39. These dispatches without the enclosures are printed in Turne *CFM,* II, 244–73. All are dated October 5 or 7.

ably accede to the request for his recall. Not only were the Jacobins in power, but he had recently received a letter from Deforgues (Lebrun's Jacobin-appointed successor) taking him sharply to task for not observing the directives of the Washington administration and for failing to keep the French government informed about the progress of his mission.[40] Equally unsettling was the evidence that popular opinion was turning against him, for numerous resolutions had been adopted condemning him for his threat to appeal to the people. The response of the pro-French element was scarcely heartening, for the resolutions sponsored by the republican interest fell short of a full endorsement of the French Minister. Even more crushing was the news (which he received early in November) that the fleet was bound for France. This ended his hope that a dramatic coup in Canada or Louisiana would gloss over his diplomatic failures. Outwardly he maintained an air of confidence and good spirits, but Hauterive detected an inner sadness about him as well as an unaccustomed restlessness of manner. Sadly the Consul reflected that Genet's precocious talents, his early successes, and the advantages he had enjoyed in his career had all come to nothing. Being rather fond of metaphors, Hauterive likened Genet to a flourishing tree, which bore only drab flowers and whose fruits fell prematurely.[41]

There were also private reasons to give his thoughts a melancholy cast. For some time, rumors (presumably launched by the Hamiltonians) had been circulating that he had a wife and children in France. Understandably Governor Clinton, as much as he admired the Minister, refused to permit Cornelia to marry Genet until it was certain that these reports were not true.[42]

40. Dated July 30, 1793, in Turner, *CFM,* II, 228–31.

41. Hauterive MS Diary, November 16, 1793, New-York Historical Society.

42. *Ibid.,* November 13, 1793; Hugh Williamson to Alexander Hamilton, October 24, 1793, Hamilton Papers, LC; G. C. Genet, *Genet,* 40.

10

The War of the Resolutions

IN THE LATE SUMMER OF 1793, there was indeed a large-scale appeal to the people—organized not by Genet, as might have been expected, but by the very men most hostile to him and to his nation. It was the Hamiltonians who invaded the public arena, summoning citzens in the Eastern towns and cities to public meetings at which resolutions were adopted endorsing the administration policy of neutrality and condemning Genet for threatening an appeal to the people. These gatherings, which began in late July and ran through August, produced a counter movement sponsored by two of Jefferson's closest associates, James Madison and James Monroe, who organized public meetings in Virginia to adopt resolutions intended to nullify the impression created by the Hamiltonians. The result was a species of political warfare conducted by means of resolutions adopted at public meetings. For the first time since the formation of the new government, the people were directly involved in the political process.[1]

The first resolves were enacted in Boston where Stephen Higginson (a prominent merchant) and other supporters of Hamiltonian policies sponsored a meeting on July 22 at which resolutions were adopted strongly endorsing the President's

1. In this chapter, I have relied primarily on my article, "The Genet Mission and the Development of American Political Parties," *The Journal of American History,* LII (March, 1966), 725–41.

proclamation and urging that violators be rigorously punished. The Bostonians had taken this step, Higginson explained to Hamilton, to circumvent Francophile plans of arousing public support in favor of a more generous treatment of French privateers. Higginson promised the Secretary of the Treasury that the Boston resolves would be echoed in other towns. He was as good as his word. By the end of August more than twenty similar sets of resolutions had been approved in New England.[2]

The appeal to the people initiated in Boston was expanded by Hamilton, who stimulated additional meetings to adopt esolutions incorporating a condemnation of the French Minister. He embarked on this course late in July after the President decided to request Genet's recall and when it became apparent that Washington, in spite of Hamilton's most persuasive arguments, would not make his decision public. The Secretary of the Treasury determined to publicize the details of the Minister's conduct in the expectation that this revelation would undermine public sympathy for France and damage (perhaps beyond recovery) the prestige of those administration critics closely identified with the cause of France. He assumed that the public clamor generated by press reports about Genet would force the President to confirm the charges and also announce his decision to request the Minister's recall. That he was exploiting confidential cabinet discussions did not disturb him on this occasion any more than in the past when he freely imparted administration secrets to the British Minister.

Although Hamilton initiated the exposé on July 31 in his first "No Jacobin" essay, when he reported that Genet had threatened to make an appeal to the people, he left the task of nmasking the French Minister to two of his closest friends, enator Rufus King of New York and Chief Justice John Jay. They were fully briefed on the incidents surrounding the crisis ver the *Petite Democrate* during a visit to Philadelphia in July. In the expectation that Genet might challenge their revelations, Hamilton supplied his friends with a written statement detailing

2. *Ibid.*, 729; Stephen Higginson to Hamilton, July 26, 1793; yrett, *Hamilton Papers*, XIV, 127–28, Keller, "Genet Mission," 515ff.

the circumstances which led to the Minister's threat, but not including the President's decision to request his recall.[3]

Rufus King, who returned to New York before Jay, put the machinery in motion by allowing his political associates to circulate rumors about Genet. He also arranged for the New York Chamber of Commerce to approve resolves (on August 6) praising Washington's proclamation of neutrality and condemning attempts of foreign diplomats to communicate with the nation other than through the executive branch of the government. Two days later, at King's behest, a public assembly adopted resolutions restricted to an approval of the policy of neutrality.[4] Although he had arranged for these gatherings, King was not at all happy at the notion of involving the people so directly in governmental affairs. Such meetings reminded him all too vividly of the tumults of the early years of the American Revolution and of the more recent mob disorders in France. Now that the United States had adopted a Constitution granting effective power to the central government he did not think, as he confided to Hamilton, that the nation expected the executive to "sit with folded arms, and that the Government be carried on by town meetings, and those irregular measures which disorganize Society, destroy the salutary influence of regular Government and render the Magistracy a meer [*sic*] Pageant."[5]

The New York meetings were only the beginning. By the end of the month resolutions condemning appeals to the people by foreign diplomats were adopted in New Jersey, Delaware, Virginia, and Maryland. The Burlington, New Jersey, resolves were enacted under the distinguished patronage of a revolutionary hero, General Joseph Bloomfield, while Colonel John Bayard lent his name to those adopted in New Brunswick. The

3. Frank Monaghan, *John Jay* (New York, 1955), 354–55; Hamilton to King, August 13, 1793, Syrett, *Hamilton Papers,* XIV, 239–41.

4. New York *Diary,* August 7, 1793; New York *Journal,* August 10, 1793.

5. King to Hamilton, August 3, 1793, Hamilton Papers, LC.

latter were noteworthy as the only resolves to mention Genet by name; the others adhered to the pattern set by the New York Chamber of Commerce.[6]

The charges against Genet were given greater substance on August 12 when Jay and King published a joint statement in the New York press:

> Certain late publications render it proper for us . . . to inform the public, that a Report having reached this City from Philadelphia, that Mr. Genet, the French Minister, had said he would appeal to the people from certain Decisions of the President; we were asked on our return from that place whether he had made such a declaration. We answered that he had, and we also mentioned it to others, authorizing them to say that we had informed them.[7]

This allegation, printed over the signatures of two prominent citizens rather than in the form of the usual anonymous essay, was not to be taken lightly. Many (quite erroneously) assumed that it had presidential authorization.[8] Jay and King hoped to draw Genet into making a public denial, which would enable them to confound him by producing Hamilton's circumstantial account. In this they were disappointed. The Minister did not respond directly, and Hamilton's statement remained unpublished for the moment.

Of all the meetings condemning Genet, the most important and most widely publicized was held in Richmond on August 17. This successful invasion of Jefferson's native state can be attributed to the wide contacts Hamilton and his friends possessed throughout the nation. Not only had they inherited the bonds forged by the federalists during the conflict over the ratification of the Constitution, but the Secretary of the Treasury had subordinates in every state with whom he maintained close ties. In Richmond the point of contact was through the

6. Philadelphia *Gazette of the United States,* August 21, 28, September 4, 11, 1793.

7. New York *Diary,* August 12, 1793.

8. R. R. Livingston to Edward Livingston, August 19, 1793, Livingston Papers, New-York Historical Society; L. Cadwalader to Rufus King, August 25, 1793, King Papers, *ibid.*

district Supervisor of the Revenue, Edward Carrington, who enjoyed a confidential correspondence with his chief. It should be noted, too, that the republican interest, while dominant in the state, was never in the ascendant in Richmond, the principal mercantile center of Virginia.

The Richmond meeting, which received more publicity than any other gathering, was organized by John Marshall, Edward Carrington's brother-in-law. Although not as yet well-known outside the state, Marshall was a leading figure at the bar and a citizen of considerable influence in Richmond. He issued the call for the meeting on August 10, a full week before the Jay-King statement appeared in the local press. In a shrewd maneuver, he placed one of Jefferson's friends in the chair—the distinguished jurist George Wythe. Wythe's sponsorship led many to conclude that the resolutions had the blessing of the Secretary of State. In addition to a strong endorsement of Washington's proclamation, the Richmond resolves were outspoken in condemning all attempts by foreign diplomats to communicate with the people except through the executive. In accordance with the practice established at Northern meetings Genet was not mentioned by name.[9]

The leaders of the republican interest were unprepared for this onslaught and they rightly feared that widespread denunciation of Genet, if left unanswered, might convince Washington that the people cared little about the fate of France. James Madison and James Monroe, Jefferson's two closest political associates, took the first steps to counteract the impression created by the recent meetings. By a happy accident Madison was visiting Monroe at his Albemarle County home (about seventy miles west of Richmond) when they first saw the report of the Richmond meeting and read the text of the Jay-King statement. They realized that immediate action was necessary, but they had no time to consult Jefferson who was still in the capital. The fact that Genet had been guilty of an indiscretion did not come as a surprise. For some time they had been aware of Jef-

9. Ammon, "Genet Mission," *loc. cit.*, LII, 732.

ferson's dissatisfaction with the French Minister, for the Secretary of State kept them informed of cabinet discussions—a confidence they scrupulously respected—but they failed to grasp the seriousness of the situation. Primarily concerned with private affairs, they had not sensed the mounting tone of anxiety in Jefferson's letters. Moreover, Madison apparently assumed that political controversies, as in the past, would not reach a critical stage until Congress met. Only then would the issues be drawn and the parties arrayed for combat.[10]

It so happened that Madison had with him a letter written by Jefferson on August 3 informing him about the decision to recall Genet. The Secretary of State had also warned Madison that Genet would "*sink the republican interest* if they do *not abandon him.*" [11] The crucial passages (here italicized) were composed in a personal cipher frequently used by Jefferson, who suspected Hamilton of having spies in the postal service. Unfortunately, Madison, who had left his key to the cipher in Fredericksburg, had not been able to decode Jefferson's letter.

Consequently, as Madison and Monroe examined the resolutions approved in Richmond and in Northern towns, their first reaction was that the Anglophiles had seized on some trivial incident and were inflating it out of all proportion to undermine popular affection for France. It was in this light that Monroe penned hasty notes to his friends warning them:

> The monarchy party among [us] has seized a new ground whereon to advance their fortunes. The French minister has been guilty, in the vehemence of his zeal, of some indiscretion, slighting the President of the United States, and instead of healing the breach, this party have brought it to the public view and are labouring to turn the popularity of this respectable citizen, against the French revolution, thinking to separate us from France and pave the way for an unnatural connection with Great Britain. Jay and King have certified the indiscretion charged to the minister, and handed it to the public printers. I have time only to suggest the idea, to enable

10. *Ibid.*, 733.
11. Ford, *Jefferson*, VI, 361–62.

you to understand what you may see in relation to this object, and to put the friends of republican government on their guard.[12]

Considering it essential that there be some new proof of public attachment to France, Madison and Monroe decided to organize a series of meetings in Virginia under the "auspices of respectable names" to bring out, what Madison termed, "the real sense of the people." [13] By August 25, they had completed a model set of resolutions, which opened with a preamble reflecting their distrust of the mercantile community. Additional resolves were needed, they said, to show that the views of the people living in the country were radically different from those of the town dwellers who could more easily assemble to voice their opinions. After praising Washington for his patriotic service to the nation and his devotion to peace, the resolutions continued with an expression of the gratitude Americans felt towards France for her assistance in the past and of their sympathy for America's ally now engaged in a similar struggle for liberty. The resolutions concluded by asserting that the men trying to alienate the two republics hoped to make the United States an ally of Great Britain as the first step in the establishment of a monarchy. Of the truth of these charges there could be no doubt in view of the "active zeal displayed by persons . . . . of known Monarch[ica]l principles." [14] Since they had no information about Genet's conduct, Madison and Monroe wisely avoided all reference to the Minister in their draft.

They had barely finished the draft, when a letter arrived from Jefferson, which made immediate revision essential. The Secretary of State, as soon as he learned that Madison did not have the key to his cipher, sent an account of Genet's misbehavior by a special messenger, who caught up with Madison at Monroe's plantation on August 28. With the full story before them, they realized that the resolutions must disengage the republican interest from the Minister. Monroe, a far more ardent

12. Monroe to John Breckinridge, August 23, 1793, Emmett Collection, New York Public Library.

13. August 27, 1793, James Madison, *Writings* (9 vols., New York 1900–10), Gaillard Hunt, ed., VI, 179.

14. For a copy of the resolves see *ibid.,* VI, 192, fn. 1.

Francophile than Madison, was unwilling to repudiate Genet, for this would surely give the victory to the Hamiltonians. Eventually they agreed not to denounce him specifically, but to expand the final resolution with a statement affirming the general principle that foreign diplomats must conduct their negotiations with the executive and condemning appeals to the people. This passage was further modified (probably as a concession to Monroe) by a clause stating that if the French Minister did make an appeal to the people, it would be regarded as a reflection on him and not on his nation.[15] The additions made after receiving Jefferson's letter gave the Madison-Monroe resolves a distant resemblance to those sponsored by the Hamiltonians, but they differed in the stress Madison and Monroe placed on friendship with France and by their avoidance of an explicit endorsement of the President's policy of neutrality.

Their task completed, Madison returned home, leaving Monroe to promote the adoption of the resolves throughout the state by enlisting the cooperation of friends. Thus John Taylor obliged by sponsoring a meeting in Caroline County with his uncle Edmund Pendleton in the chair. Pendleton's presence added a special cachet to the Caroline resolves, for he was a revered revolutionary leader and an old friend of the President. Since they did not have contacts in every part of the state, Monroe turned to the press. In a series of essays signed "Agricola," Monroe urged the citizens of Virginia to come forward and declare their affection for France. Making no effort to refute the charges against the French Minister, he took the offensive by questioning the motives of those seeking to discredit Genet. All, according to Monroe, were "enemies of the French Revolution, who are likewise notoriously partisans for monarchy." As Agricola hammered away on this theme (there were four numbers in all), John Marshall (disguised as "Gracchus" and "Aristides") replied denying that Genet's critics were secret monarchists. As a result of Monroe's endeavors at least a dozen

15. Ammon, "Genet Mission," *loc cit.*, LII, 735.

sets of resolves were adopted in Virginia by the end of October.[16]

Resolutions along the lines of the Madison-Monroe model
were not enacted outside Virginia. In other states the conflict was confined to the press. The lack of a more general
public movement in behalf of France can be attributed to several factors. In the first place, the Virginia spokesmen did not
have as effective interstate connections as the Hamiltonians
As far as can be ascertained, they made no effort to enlist the
support of the Clintonians in New York, or of friends such as
Mifflin and Dallas in Pennsylvania, either because they were
unsure of the response, or (and this is more likely) because
they expected the example of Virginia to evoke a similar re-
ponse in other states.

The most significant factor in curtailing the war of the resolutions must be ascribed to circumstances, which, in an earlier
age, would have been labeled an act of God—the devastating
outbreak of yellow fever in Philadelphia.[17] Although the firs
cases had been detected in July, the disease did not achieve
epidemic proportions until the end of August, when all who
could fled the city. In mid-October, when the death rate soared
to nearly a hundred a day, the only residents still in the capita
were working-men and their families, servants, blacks, a few
government and civic officials, and a handful of dedicated
physicians including the celebrated Dr. Benjamin Rush. By thi
time governmental operations were largely suspended, all news
papers but one had ceased publication and little mail was for
warded. As the panic spread to the seaboard cities and to the
towns near Philadelphia, stages from the capital were denied
passage and refugees were not permitted entrance. Unde
these circumstances public meetings were discouraged. Th
suspension of the newspapers prevented the Virginia resolve
from receiving a wide circulation, for the Philadelphia pres

16. *Ibid.*, 736.

17. See J. H. Powell, *Bring Out Your Dead: The Great Plague o Yellow Fever in Philadelphia in 1793* (Philadelphia, 1949), 220–2 238–54, 266–69, 281.

functioned as a clearing house for news from all parts of the Union. In an era of scissors-and-paste journalism the press in the capital fulfilled the same function as a modern wire service. Not until the first snowfall early in December did Philadelphians feel out of danger and the city return to normal. At least 4,000 persons out of a population of 55,000 perished during the epidemic.

The Virginia resolves achieved only a limited circulation, but they were seen by one most important person—Washington. His replies to the addresses accompanying the resolves from both camps were invariably noncommittal messages thanking the citizens for their commendation of his past record and expressing general agreement with their sentiments of gratitude for France's aid during the American Revolution. It must have given Hamilton considerable pleasure when Washington asked him to draft a reply to the address submitted by John Marshall's Richmond meeting. Hamilton departed from the President's usual formula only in that he omitted all references to France's past assistance.[18]

If Washington was able to exhibit a calm, nonpartisan tone in his public utterances, his private reaction was quite different, for he resented the implied criticism of his policy in the resolves adopted under the aegis of Madison and Monroe. He voiced his feelings about Genet in a letter to Richard Henry Lee late in October. "The best that can be said of this agent," he told Lee, "is that he is entirely unfit for the Mission on which he is employed, unless, contrary to the express and unequivocal declaration of his Country (which I hope is not the case) . . . it is meant to involve ours in all the horrors of a European War. This, or interested motives of his own, or being become the dupe and tool of a Party formed on various principles, but to effect local purposes, is the only solution that can be given to his conduct." [19] From this letter it is apparent that Washington by

18. Washington received the Richmond address while he was still in Philadelphia. Washington to Hamilton, August 27, 1793, Hamilton Papers, LC; New York *Daily Advertiser,* September 26, 1793.

19. October 24, 1793, Fitzpatrick, *Washington* XXXIII, 138.

the end of 1793 was no longer a neutral in the party conflict, but had committed himself fully to the Hamiltonian position. The President's hypersensitivity to criticism (a characteristic known to all his associates) was blinding him to the fact that the motives of those supporting his policies were just as much open to question as the objectives of those in opposition. Washington was so concious of his own integrity and so utterly convinced that his decisions were based on highest considerations of national interest that he could not admit the possibility of a more flexible policy of neutrality, which would not only be more acceptable to the people but would not endanger Anglo-American relations.

Genet's contributions to the press during the furore stirred up by the Jay-King revelations provided little consolation for his supporters. His letter of August 13 to Washington was not only rude but it left unanswered the basic questions raised by Jay and King.[20] Moreover, most agreed that it would be improper for the President to involve himself in a partisan dispute. Nor did Genet's letter to Governor Moultrie, published in the New York press on October 25, do much to clarify the situation. It was a reply to a letter from Moultrie (received a month earlier) asking about the veracity of the charges. Avoiding a precise denial Genet assured Moultrie that he would have long since exposed these "falsehoods, which a dark and deep intrigue has laid to my charge, if I could have condescended to put myself on a level with those men whom I too much despise to produce proof against the absurdity of their accusations." He then sought to create the impression that the most he had ever contemplated was a vindication of his conduct through Congressional action. "It is to Congress," he continued, "that I shall address myself through the medium of the executive of the United States, to ask the severest examination of my official measures, and of every step which may be supposed to have been an attempt upon the established Authority of the Ameri-

20. See pp. 118–19 above.

can Republic. . . ." He promised to conceal nothing, for he would publish all his correspondence with the administration, the French government and the consuls. From these documents the public would be able to see that if he had spoken to the administration "with the energy of a freeman, with the enthusiasm which inspires and animates every Frenchman really attached to his country," he had never forgotten the respect due the President.[21]

A few days later Genet released an ill-tempered letter to Jefferson protesting the revocation of the powers of the French Consul in Boston, Antoine C. Duplaine, who had used armed forces from a French warship to rescue a privateer which he had outfitted from the custody of local authorities. This, it might be added, was but the last of a long series of violations of American neutrality committed by Duplaine. Genet denounced Washington's action as contrary to the Constitution of the United States, which has "empowered him, as first Minister of the American people, to admit and receive the Ministers of foreign nations . . ." but had not given him the authority to discharge them. Only the nation sending diplomatic agents had the power of dismissal. Insolently he continued: "I do not recollect what the worm eating [*sic*] writings of Grotius, Puffendorf and Vattel say. . . . I thank God I have forgot what these hired jurisprudents have written on the rights of nations, at a period when they were all enchained." [22]

Genet's friends were dismayed by these ill-conceived effusions in the press. Robert Livingston, now quite disillusioned with the Minister, felt that Genet's "intemperate warmth" would work to the injury of the "republican interest" in New York. Alexander J. Dallas, once a friend and genuine admirer, was equally exasperated by the Minister's lack of common sense. "Genet's conduct," he wrote Albert Gallatin, "is really extravagant. I do not so much object to his matter as his manner of complaint. I think, amidst all his rant about the rights of man, I can discern a care about self. . . . Every step that

21. Genet to Moultrie, October 15, 1793, in *ibid.*, Oct. 23, 1793.
22. Genet to Jefferson, October 27, 1793, in *ibid.*, October 31, 1793.

Genet has taken seems a greater display of vanity than talents, and leaves us, who love his cause, to deplore that he was deputed to support it. I am afraid that he alone is not to blame, however, for the nature of his reception elated and bewildered him; and we should have calculated upon the possibility of his mistaking a zealous attachment to the end, for a licentious disposition to adopt any means which he should think subservient to it." He asked Gallatin, who was in New York, to talk to Genet, not that it was "in the power of any man to influence" the French Minister, but at least he should be warned of the danger to which he was exposing himself.[23]

The Minister's admirers would have been still more appalled had they seen some of his unpublished correspondence with the Secretary of State, for the Minister was immersed in a bitter wrangle resulting from his failure to address requests for the accreditation of consuls to the President of the United States. Ever since his arrival Genet had accredited consuls to the Congress of the United States. The matter had been called to his attention on a number of occasions, but he persisted, for it was now part and parcel of his contention that Congress was the true sovereign of the nation. In October Jefferson notified Genet that consular appointments would not be recognized unless the credentials were addressed to the President. Genet's acknowledgement was a promise to "enlighten" his government with Jefferson's "judicious reflections," but until he received further instructions he would continue to accredit them to Congress. This combination of defiance and sarcasm, even on such a trivial issue, was too much. At Washington's explicit orders, the Secretary of State penned a sharp response, affirming the position of the administration and reminding the Minister that it was not within the power of a foreign diplomat to become "umpire and judge" of constitutional questions nor to "*personally*" question the President's authority.[24] Much of Genet's

23. R. R. Livingston to Edward Livingston, November 11, 1793, Livingston Papers, New-York Historical Society; Dallas to Gallatin, November 8, 1793, Gallatin Papers, *ibid.*

24. Jefferson to Genet, October 2, November 22, 1793, Genet to Jefferson, November 14, 1793, *ASPFR,* I, 178, 184.

irritation can be attributed to his bitterness over the failure of Jefferson's friends to defend his conduct. Even those resolutions supposedly pro-French in character tacitly conceded that he had threatened an appeal to the people. Moreover, now that his recall had been requested he was concerned about the impression that his notes would have on the Jacobins. It was much to his advantage to appear as the stout champion of republicanism against the aristocratic Washington administration.

As far as the immediate objectives of the Hamiltonians were concerned, the outcome of the appeal to the public was disappointing, for the President did not reveal the news of his decision to request Genet's recall. Nor did the charges against Genet have the anticipated devastating effect upon the pro-French party. In the absence of official confirmation, the Francophile publicists were able to argue that the accusations against the Minister were nothing but slanders circulated by the monarchical party. This was not the most effective reply, but it served to blunt the impact of the charges. There was undoubtedly some erosion in the ranks of the pro-French party, as moderates, appalled by the Minister's rudeness to the President, joined the Hamiltonians. The war of the resolutions settled one important issue—the extent of popular support for Washington's neutrality policy. It was now clear that the people, while still concerned about the success of the French Revolution and grateful for France's assistance in the past, accepted without question the administration interpretation of American treaty obligations. In organizing public meetings to endorse the proclamation and publicize Genet's misconduct, Hamilton and his associates had demonstrated that new forces could be used to achieve political ends. It was a lesson which the republican leaders learned better than their opponents. During the balance of the decade of the 1790s, public assemblies played a major role in the attack on the Federalist Party all the way from Jay's Treaty to the Alien and Sedition Acts.

In practical terms the new patterns of political behavior exposed the need to improve interstate political contacts and also to establish closer relations with the voter other than just at election time. There was also a change in voter attitudes. Citizens were now expected to participate more actively in politics and to express their views in a manner calculated to influence the final decision. The new involvement of the voters constituted an essential step in the democratization of American politics and in the formation of the first parties, which emerged as distinct entities during the next two years. The conflict over Genet had still another important consequence—it made neutrality in politics virtually impossible. The issues presented by the outbreak of the war between France and Great Britain, the French Revolution, and the Minister's conduct, compelled men to take sides. They could no longer function as independents deciding each question on its merits, for all political issues had to be evaluated in the light of a set of basic ideological commitments.

11

Denouement

IN VIEW OF the bitter infighting within the Washington administration, the violent public controversy over Genet's conduct and the Minister's belligerent attitude, the final scenes of his mission seem curiously anticlimactic. After all the fuss and fury during the previous six months the basic issues still remained largely unresolved. Neither the enemies nor the friends of France had managed to win a clear-cut victory. While Washington's foreign policy was clearly influenced by Hamilton's views, it still fell short of the ultimate goal contemplated by the Secretary of the Treasury. Genet himself behaved with unexpected restraint. He was not even on hand when Congress assembled in Philadelphia on December 3. By the time he arrived ten days later, the President's message announcing the request for his recall was appearing in the Eastern press. Genet's much discussed appeal was presented in a form lacking his usual dramatic flair, and consequently it aroused only the mildest ripple of comment. The real drama was provided by the President's special message which was accompanied by Genet's correspondence. These documents, exposing for the first time the rude and insolent conduct of the Minister, produced much unfavorable commentary but few defenses, for the friends of France had long since ceased attempting to justify Genet's demands. The materials released by the President satisfied public curiosity on every point but one—the question of the threat to appeal to the people. Since Washington had not included Jefferson's report of July 10, which he considered an internal administration paper, the matter remained a subject for public controversy.

Although the Congressional session was not scheduled until the beginning of December, the President left Mount Vernon at the end of October to meet the cabinet members at Germantown, Pennsylvania. He had chosen this site, just a few miles from the capital, as a convenient location for ascertaining whether the yellow fever epidemic would make it necessary to select another location for the session. He had already consulted Jefferson (who in turn conferred with Madison) on this point. Jointly they advised him that it must convene in Philadelphia. Since the other secretaries were of a contrary opinion, Washington postponed a decision until he could examine conditions in Philadelphia.[1] This conflict was never resolved, for the epidemic subsided with the arrival of cooler weather. The President and the Secretaries remained in Germantown during November while messengers scurried back and forth from the capital fetching copies of the documents needed for the President's messages. There were several messages under preparation. The first, to be read at the opening session on December 3, was devoted to a general review of the past year. Corresponding to the modern State of the Union message, it was then known as the President's speech. The second message (submitted December 5) was restricted to American relations with France and Great Britain. Other less important messages (submitted later in the month) were devoted to relations with Spain, Portugal, and the Barbary states.[2]

In the course of the numerous cabinet meetings in Germantown, the contents of the speech and the special message were extensively discussed without exposing any new points of view. The Secretaries still differed on the same issues, but at least ex-

1. Malone, *Jefferson,* III, 144–45; Powell, *Bring Out Your Dead,* 264–73.

2. Reprinted in *Messages and Papers of the Presidents 1789–1897,* James D. Richardson, ed. (11 vols., Washington, D. C., 1875–93), I, 138–49.

pressed their opinions less acrimoniously than earlier in the year. The only perceptible change in the internal relations among the cabinet members was that Randolph who was to become Secretary of State at the end of the year, supported Jefferson much more strongly than in the past. Thus when Washington at an early meeting suggested the possibility of dismissing Genet immediately, Randolph agreed with Jefferson that nothing should be done, since news of his recall could be expected shortly. Washington concurred, although, as Jefferson noted, he obviously "felt the venom of Genet's pen." [3]

The most important disagreement occurred over the manner in which the President should present the April proclamation in his speech to Congress. Hamilton, adhering to the position outlined in his "Pacificus" essays, wished it to be regarded as an official statement of national policy effectively barring future demands under the terms of the treaties of 1778. If this approach was accepted, then Congress would not be expected to respond to the proclamation. Jefferson, on the other hand, preferred that it be presented as an expression of the President's opinion, and therefore not binding as a policy declaration. Washington's statement, drafted by Randolph, avoided both these extremes. The proclamation was introduced as a measure necessary to "admonish our citizens of the consequences of a contraband trade and of hostile acts" against the belligerents and at the same time obtain "by a declaration of the existing legal state of things an easier admission of our right to the immunities belonging to our situation." Once again the dread word neutrality was avoided. The President informed Congress of the administration rules concerning belligerents, recommending that they be incorporated into the penal laws of the United States to facilitate enforcement. The President also suggested that American citizens be barred from enlisting in foreign military or naval services.[4] It is not surprising, in view of the recent public demonstrations in support of the proclamation, that these passages in Washington's speech were singled

3. Jefferson, *Anas,* November 8, 1793, Ford, *Jefferson,* I, 266.
4. *Messages,* Richardson, ed., I, 139; Malone, *Jefferson,* III, 148.

out for especial praise by both houses in their customary replies to the President's address.

Jefferson's draft of the message on relations with France and Great Britain was approved with slight modifications. Hamilton strongly argued that there be no reference either to England's failure to execute the Treaty of Peace of 1783 or to the Order in Council of June 8, 1793, authorizing the seizure of grain, flour, and other foodstuffs on neutral vessels bound for French ports. Since the latter measure had aroused a burst of indignation throughout the country, Jefferson considered it only fair to include it as a counterbalance to the unfavorable observations on Genet's conduct. Hamilton's contention that these items should be reserved for a special secret message on the grounds that they were subjects of pending negotiations did not impress Washington, who accepted Jefferson's opinion that they should be included. The only concession made to Hamilton was the elimination of phrases intended to soften the request for Genet's recall. Thus a passage expressing gratitude to France for "favors ancient and recent" was eliminated. Nonetheless, Jefferson succeeded in wording the message so that the request for Genet's recall rested on his offensive conduct and was not to be interpreted as an act hostile to France. "It is with extreme concern," the President informed the Senate, "that I have to inform you that the proceedings of the person . . . the French have unfortunately appointed their minister plenipotentiary here have breathed nothing of the friendly spirit of the nation which sent him. Their tendency, on the contrary, has been to involve us in a war abroad and anarchy at home." [5]

On the same day that the President informed the Senate of his request for Genet's recall, Jay and King renewed their attack on the Minister by publishing in *Dunlap's American Advertiser* of Philadelphia a detailed account of the circumstances surrounding Genet's threat to appeal to the people. This statement (based on data supplied by Hamilton in August) carried

5. *Messages,* Richardson, ed., I, 146; Malone, *Jefferson,* III, 149–50.

a note signed by Hamilton and Knox certifying the accuracy of its contents. The object of the renewed onslaught was to force the President to release Jefferson's report of July 10 which would confirm the charges against Genet. In the same issue of the paper, the editor inserted a notice that Alexander J. Dallas, who allegedly heard Genet make his threat, was preparing a statement. Dallas's letter, which appeared on December 9, was, to put it mildly, equivocal, or, as Jay aptly commented, "artful." Dallas admitted that Genet had spoken of an appeal, but he flatly denied that the Minister intended appealing to the people over the head of the President. What Genet had meant, according to Dallas, was to appeal to Congress by publishing his correspondence with the executive. Dallas, who had Monroe's aid in composing his letter, managed to create the impression that Hamilton and Knox had deliberately circulated an erroneous story obtained from a third party (Governor Mifflin) instead of asking Dallas, whom they saw every day, for a correct version. As soon as Monroe realized that Dallas was not going to substantiate the charges made against Genet, he wrote Jefferson advising him to remain silent in the dispute. The warning was timely, for Jefferson was considering publication of his report of July 10. He gladly followed Monroe's advice, which coincided with his own distaste for direct involvement in newspaper polemics.[6]

Hamilton made one last attempt to force the publication of Jefferson's report. On December 17 an anonymous writer asserted in the *Dunlap's American Advertiser* that on July 8 Jefferson had informed Hamilton of Genet's threat to appeal to the people. This announcement, drafted by the Secretary of the Treasury, was worded so skillfully that the casual reader might infer that Jefferson had supplied the item. The next day, undoubtedly in response to protests, the editor identified Knox and Hamilton as his informants. At this point, as far as the public was concerned, the matter rested, leaving the question of the truth or fallacy of the Jay-King charges an open question.

6. Ammon, "Genet Mission," *loc. cit.*, LII, 739; Monroe to Jefferson, December 4, 1793, Hamilton, *Monroe*, I, 279.

Genet, who appeared in Philadelphia on December 12, now injected himself into the controversy. On December 16, he wrote the Attorney General demanding that Jay and King be prosecuted for libel. When he first made this request a month earlier, Randolph had suggested that they discuss the question after Genet's return to the capital. Acting on Washington's instructions, the Attorney General prepared a formal reply to the Minister's second request, informing him that prosecutions of this nature could not be undertaken by the government but must be instituted through a civil suit. Although the Minister consulted Peter S. Duponceau and Joseph Thomas (prominent attorneys with republican affiliations), who assured him that he did indeed have a case, he never brought suit against Jay and King. For once Genet heeded the advice of those who knew all too well that the Minister would lose his case if the defendants produced Jefferson's report.

Jay and King were understandably indignant over the threatened suit. It was scarcely appropriate for the Chief Justice of the United States and a Senator to have made charges about the conduct of a diplomat—charges, as republican writers in the press happily pointed out, which remained totally unsubstantiated. Their sense of outrage was all the greater since they knew that their accusations were confirmed by Jefferson's report. In their determination to vindicate themselves, Jay and King were willing to risk the President's displeasure by bringing direct pressure to force him to release Jefferson's report. In January, they jointly wrote Washington protesting the continued silence of the administration and commenting acidly upon Jefferson's duplicity. Washington considered their letter offensive, but rather than alienate two such influential men, he reluctantly agreed to grant them a private interview. After several heated conferences with the President, Jay and King consented to the destruction of their letter of protest in exchange for a copy of Jefferson's report of July 10. It was also agreed that the President would explain in writing his reasons for maintaining silence on the charges against Genet.

On February 21—the day Genet's successor arrived—

King (Jay was in New York) called on the President bearing all the copies of the letter of protest. The President then solemnly read a statement justifying his conduct, which was burned along with the copies of the letter written by Jay and King. The Senator from New York received, as he had been promised, a copy of Jefferson's report with the understanding that it would only be used in the event of a libel prosecution. Since Genet never brought suit, Jefferson's statement reposed quietly among Rufus King's private papers.[7]

Apart from the publication of the letter demanding that Jay and King be prosecuted for libel, Genet's performance was far short of the dramatic confrontation suggested in a letter to the Foreign Minister written on December 10, 1793, just before he left New York. He was (he had informed his chief) departing for the capital, ready for "mortal combat" with his enemies. If Congress (and this he considered improbable) failed to do him justice, then he would attack "Washington himself in the Federal Court and force him to appear at the bar" to defend his policies. Of all the many absurdities propounded by the French Minister, this was perhaps the most preposterous. Did he seriously think he could hail the President before a court presided over by John Jay, or was he merely trying to impress the Jacobins with his unrelenting struggle on behalf of France's interests? In spite of these bold statements, this dispatch (which proved to be his last) was less flamboyant than his earlier ones.[8]

After his arrival in Philadelphia, Genet busied himself with ceremonial calls on members of the administration and on Congressmen. Among those so honored was Vice President John Adams. Although Adams was out at the time of the Minister's visit, he was sufficiently curious about this notorious revolu-

7. Ammon, "Genet Mission," *loc. cit.,* 739–40; Keller, "Genet Mission," 541–49; Frank Monaghan, *John Jay* (New York, 1935), 358–59; Statement of Rufus King, February 1794, Charles King, *Life of Rufus King,* I, 474–78; letters in Genet Papers, LC.

8. December 10, 1793, Turner, *CFM,* II, 277–79.

tionary firebrand and son of an old friend to return the call. His reaction was not entirely unfavorable. As he told his daughter, Genet appeared to be a "young gentleman of much ingenuity, lively wit and brilliant imagination, enamoured to distraction with republican liberty; very crude and inaccurate in his ideas of a republic and as yet totally uninformed about the operations of the human heart and the progress of the passions in public assemblies." It seemed to him that Genet had been very much misled by the opponents of the administration.[9]

Genet had no reason to complain about the reception given him by the Congressmen associated with the republican interest, for they seemed as cordial as they had been in the past. Madison and William Branch Giles (a young Virginian and a leading spokesman of anti-administration forces in the House) dined with the Minister. Yet this friendliness was without significance, for none was prepared to endorse his conduct or seek to reverse administration foreign policy through Congressional action. By maintaining an outward but noncommittal cordiality, they merely wished to avoid giving the impression that they were hostile to France or that they believed the Jay-King charges to be true. Although Genet felt that most Congressmen were aware of the correctness of his interpretation of France's treaty rights, he quickly realized that he could not find support within the halls of Congress. As he confided to Cornelia, everyone was so in awe of Washington that none dared raise a cry against the administration.[10]

Genet's appeal to Congress was a disappointing production —a twenty-four page pamphlet containing a translation of his instructions and a few letters relevant to his mission. Except for the instructions, from which he excised all references to the liberation of Louisiana and Canada, the publication offered nothing new, for the President had previously released the letters.

9. To A. A. Smith, December 14, 1793, Roof, *Col. Smith and Lady*, 220–21.

10. Genet to Cornelia, December 17, 24, 1793, Genet Papers, New-York Historical Society Genet to Cornelia, December 25, 1793, Genet Papers, LC.

The notes selected by Genet were those which placed France in the best possible light. They dealt with the proffered commercial treaty and the protests he had made about British violations of American neutrality on the high seas. On December 20, Genet requested Jefferson to transmit his publication to Congress. The response, written on December 31 (Jefferson's last day in office), was a terse refusal. The Secretary of State informed Genet that the President was the sole judge of materials to be submitted to the legislature. Once again he reminded the Minister that all official business must be conducted through the executive. After this rebuff, Genet released the documents to the public, but only the instructions were widely reprinted.[11] While they did not excite much public comment, many Americans undoubtedly shared George Hammond's opinion that "however intemperate his conduct may have been, he had not essentially exceeded the spirit of his instructions." Even Genet cannot have seriously believed his own assurances to Cornelia that the documents were having a great impact.[12] A few meetings were held denouncing the anti-French policy of the administration and praising France for the generous offer of a new commercial treaty, but these were the work of extreme groups such as the Democratic Republican Society of Philadelphia and not representative of public opinion. Few Americans were prepared to challenge policies sanctioned by the revered Washington.[13]

The news of Genet's recall reached Philadelphia in mid-January, three months after his dismissal by the Committee of

11. Keller, "Genet Mission," 552–54; Jefferson to Genet, December 31, 1793, *Writings of Thomas Jefferson,* A. Lipscomb and Albert Berg, eds. (20 vols., Washington, D. C., 1900–04), IX, 277–78.

12. Hammond to Grenville, February 22, 1794, cited in Woodfin, "Genet Mission," 485. Governor Clinton made a similar comment to Cornelia, January 15, 1794, Genet Papers, New-York Historical Society. See also Genet to Cornelia, January 1, 1794, *ibid.*

13. Philadelphia resolutions dated January 9, 1794, are in Genet Papers, LC. Another set approved on January 1 in Ulster County, New York (Clinton's home county), at a meeting presided over by James Nicholson are in *ibid.*

Public Safety, which now held supreme power. The messenger bearing Jefferson's letter to Morris reached Paris early in October. On October 11, three days after Morris delivered the American protest, the Committee agreed to recall Genet.[14] Although the Committee condemned Genet's conduct and ordered the disarming of the privateers he had outfitted, the Committee's action did not reflect a profound dissatisfaction with the Minister. When the Jacobins came to power in the summer of 1793, Genet's mission had been scrutinized, for he was naturally suspect as a Girondin appointee. Although the Jacobin Minister of Foreign Affairs had reprimanded him on July 30 for not observing proper forms in his dealings with the American government and for failing to provide detailed reports of his conferences with the Secretary of State, it was not thought necessary to remove a citizen whose patriotism was unquestioned. The Committee members realized he had acted impulsively and misinterpreted his public reception, yet they fully agreed with his conclusion about the pro-British and aristocratic character of the Washington administration. They accepted as axiomatic his contention that France could not expect to have a government in America friendly to her interests until the pro-French party obtained power.[15]

The Jacobins were in no mood to coddle a nation which declined to support France in her struggle for liberty and failed to observe existing treaty obligations. Jacobin irritation at American policy had been apparent earlier in the year in the order of July 27, 1793, authorizing the seizure of neutral ships bound for enemy ports with cargoes of foodstuffs. Technically a retaliation against the British Orders in Council of June, it was a clear indication that the Jacobins were unwilling to continue the privileged status enjoyed by the United States. The changed

14. October 18, 1793, *The Diary and Letters of Gouverneur Morris* Ann Cary Morris, ed. (2 vols., New York, 1888), II, 54.

15. See the report on Genet to the Committee of Public Safety Turner, *CFM,* II, 283–86; Thomas Paine to Barère, September 9, 1793 AECPEU; Paul Mantoux, "Le Comité de salut publique et la mission de Genet aux États-Unis," *Revue d'histoire moderne et contemporaine* XIII, 10–13.

attitude was made more pointed later in the summer when all American ships in Bordeaux were placed under an embargo.[16] This was a particularly unfriendly gesture since these vessels had risked British seizure to bring provisions to France. These measures marked the beginning of a harder line towards the United States which characterized French policy until Napoleon came to power.

In view of Jacobin resentment, it is unlikely that Genet would have been recalled had not national interest dictated acquiescence. In October, 1793, France's need for supplies was greater than ever for the Convention was raising a conscript army nearly half a million strong. It was imperative to continue friendly relations with the Washington administration—France could not risk a quarrel with a potential granary. The Jacobins also hoped that French diplomats resident in America would be instrumental in bringing the republican element to power and thus establish a regime friendly to France. Under these circumstances the sacrifice of a former Girondin (though admittedly a patriot) seemed not only expedient but a small price to pay for the national interest of France. Moreover, the American request offered an ideal opportunity to secure the long sought removal of Gouverneur Morris, as a *quid pro quo* for dismissing Genet.

As far as Genet's future career was concerned, the request for his recall arrived at a most unfortunate time. The Jacobins had just embarked on the systematic liquidation of all opposition, a move considered necessary for France's salvation. In October the people of France had been whipped into a frenzy over the real and imagined crimes of counter-revolutionaries, traitors, and monarchists, as the Jacobins set the stage for the trial of the Queen (she was executed on October 16) and for the trial of Brissot and twenty other Girondin leaders. The trial of the Girondins was brief—they were condemned on October 30 and executed the following day. Since some justification for Genet's removal other than expediency must be offered to the

16. DeConde, *Entangling Alliance,* 400–02.

nation, the Jacobins were conveniently able to discredit him by linking him with the Girondins. He could not be accused of all their many crimes, for he had been so long absent from France, but he could be pilloried (and this was but one of the many charges leveled against the Girondins) as a secret counter-revolutionary hired by the agents of William Pitt to destroy the republic from within. A Jacobin hack issued a pamphlet accusing Genet of deliberately provoking a crisis between France and the United States to alienate the two countries and ensure American support for Great Britain. He was also depicted as an advocate of free trade, which, in the Jacobin rubric, was but another of Pitt's schemes to undermine the republic by opening France's colonies to the trade of all nations. A lesser charge was that of profiting from purchases made on France's behalf. All this may seem absurd, but in the atmosphere of France at that time, no one questioned the veracity of these accusations.

Not until after the publication of the pamphlet and the execution of the Girondins did Robespierre rise in the National Convention on November 17 to denounce Genet in much the same terms as the hired pamphleteer. He made one other shocking disclosure about the machinations of the Girondins—there was still another traitor in the diplomatic service in America, a brother-in-law of Brissot who had been given a consular appointment.[17]

The principal figure on the four-man commission sent to replace Genet was Jean Fauchet, who bore the title of Minister Plenipotentiary. As head of the mission, he seems to have generally controlled policy in spite of frequent disagreements with his colleagues. All the members of the commission were relatively obscure minor functionaries without previous diplomatic experience. Fauchet, the most distinguished of the four, had held administrative posts in the war department and in the office of the Mayor of Paris. In choosing such comparatively un-

17. Keller, "Genet Mission," 496–99; Mantoux, "Mission de Genet," *loc cit.*, XIII, 18–27; Frederick Jackson Turner, "Documents on the Relations of France to Louisiana," *American Historical Review* III, 507, fn. 1.

distinguished men and linking them in a joint responsibility, the Committee of Public Safety was both de-emphasizing the importance of the American mission and making it impossible for a strong-minded individual, like Genet, to embark independently on policies potentially embarrassing to the French government.

The instructions for Fauchet and the commissioners, couched in more restrained language than those given Genet, defined the principal object of the mission as the restoration of good relations with the United States. To achieve this the commissioners were authorized to disavow Genet, disarm his privateers, curtail (if there was time) the expedition against Louisiana, and propose, as a token of France's sincerity of purpose, a new treaty of commerce on a broad base of reciprocity. Yet, while prepared to make these concessions the commissioners were to insist on a strict observance of the commercial treaty of 1778, particularly those passages permitting French prizes to be taken into American ports. In one sense the instructions were contradictory, for they expected the commissioners to win the confidence of Washington and at the same time work to destroy English influence and make France's views better known to Americans through articles in the press and through cooperation with Americans devoted to the cause of liberty. Just as in the past, a degree of interference in domestic affairs was countenanced. Fauchet quickly established contacts (though in a more discrete fashion than Genet) with anti-administration leaders in Congress. His lobbying activities against Jay's treaty in 1795 constituted a much more direct interference in American domestic politics than anything undertaken by his predecessor.[18]

Although Fauchet was ready to sail late in November contrary winds delayed him for a month, and consequently he did not reach Philadelphia until February 21, 1794. He was received by Washington the next day. During the initial stages of his residence, the new Minister made a favorable impression on

18. Instructions of November 15, 1794, Turner, *CFM,* II, 288–94; DeConde, *Entangling Alliance,* 392–98.

the President and administration supporters, who found his gravity and reserve (not just a matter of temperament—he spoke only French) more pleasing than Genet's ebullience. Moreover, he went out of his way to remove the unfavorable impression created by his predecessor by deferring to administration wishes. He accepted Washington's rulings on neutrality and preferred to devote his energies to purchasing supplies rather than in pressing for a more generous interpretation of France's treaty rights. When the President, having decided to grant Genet political asylum, refused Fauchet's request that Genet be arrested and returned to France, the new Minister did not protest. He reacted promptly to administration concern over Genet's recruiting activities in the West by issuing a proclamation canceling all commissions which had been issued. His compliance was deceptive, for Fauchet had the same opinion as Genet about the hostile character of the American government. For the moment he concealed his views, since he hoped to obtain advances on the debt and needed a free hand to purchase supplies.[19]

The new Minister treated his predecessor with exceptional consideration during the long examination of the legation accounts. Although Fauchet reported Genet's records to be in great disorder, he found no trace of misappropriation of funds. Genet was naturally relieved at the President's decision to grant him political asylum, for it seemed impossible for him to return to France in view of his identification with the Girondin conspirators. As he told Cornelia, he saw no reason for going back to a country where a despotic and vengeful government persecuted the leaders of the revolution, when he could remain in a land where virtue was honored, liberty respected and where a man who obeyed the laws had nothing to fear from tyrants or aristocrats. Cornelia's reply, which mingled declarations of love with republican enthusiasm, stirred him deeply: "How it eased my pain and renewed my heart! How beautiful

19. Commissioners to the Committee of Public Safety, May 5, 1794, Turner, *CFM*, II, 334–36.

your sentiments are, how lofty, and how Republican."[20] A few weeks after writing this letter, Genet slipped unnoticed out of the capital in mid-March for a refuge in the country.

Fauchet landed in America just in time to avert a further crisis between France and the United States over Genet's projected expeditions against Florida and Louisiana. Although rumors had been circulating for months that armed bands were being organized in Kentucky and Georgia, administration officials had no exact information about them until December when a legislative investigation in South Carolina revealed that Mangourit had issued commissions and provided funds for a force to invade Florida.

Now that Washington's policy of neutrality had received wide public endorsement, Governor Moultrie, who had originally seen nothing objectionable in the enterprise, belatedly issued a proclamation forbidding recruitment of American citizens. Although Genet inserted a letter in the Philadelphia press on December 27 denying responsibility for these activities, it is unlikely that anyone took him seriously. Just a few days later (January 4, 1794) *Dunlap's American Advertiser* printed a letter from a Western correspondent claiming that George Rogers Clark, bearing a French military commission, was raising a force to invade Louisiana. These reports nearly induced Washington to dismiss Genet summarily, but the arrival of unofficial word of the Minister's recall stayed the President's hand.[21]

The President was far more anxious about the developments in Kentucky than over the expedition sponsored by Mangourit, since reports indicated that the latter operation was small and that Moultrie would assume responsibility in checking further recruiting activities. The case of Kentucky was quite different. It seemed entirely probable that a large-scale expedition

20. Genet to Cornelia, February 24, March 1, 10, 1794, Genet Papers, New-York Historical Society. Quote is from letter of March 10.

21. Keller, "Genet Mission," 413–14; Woodfin, "Genet," 479; Rufus King, Statement of February 1794, C. King, *Rufus King,* I, 478–80; Washington to John Adams, January 8, 1794, Fitzpatrick, *Washington,* XXXIII, 234.

might be enthusiastically supported, for Westerners were deeply antagonistic toward Spain, whose refusal to open the Mississippi to American navigation threatened to blast the economic growth of the region. It was also generally accepted among the inhabitants of the West that Spain was not only failing to restrain the Indians under her control but was actually inciting them to raid the American frontier. In view of the widespread feeling that the United States government took little interest in Western affairs, it was by no means certain that state officials would do anything to prevent an invasion of Louisiana. Indeed, in the event of a conflict between the federal government and state authorities, it was always possible that the next step might be the secession of the region west of the Alleghenies. From the point of view of expediency, Washington might have preferred to ignore the rumors emanating from the West (just as he had been willing to condone Genet's plans of inciting insurrection in Louisiana), but to do so would not only place the authority of the federal government in question by approving activities contrary to his neutrality policy but also jeopardize negotiations in progress in Madrid and cloud the reputation of the new government. Like most of his contemporaries Washington felt that the United States should free itself from the politics of the Old World and seek territory by fair negotiation rather than by aggression against a weak neighbor. Hence the nervousness in Philadelphia over the reports that a force of 2,000 men (or perhaps even 6,000) was being raised. Apprehension was all the greater in view of the absence of reliable information.[22]

In January, 1794, no one in Philadelphia, least of all the French Minister, had the slightest notion of what was transpiring in Kentucky. Michaux (Genet's emissary) had not returned from his mission until December with the information that Clark was ready to raise an armed force, provided he received money for equipment. Genet had then written Clark asking that he postpone the expedition until spring in view of the

22. Richard Lowitt, "Activities of Citizen Genet in Ketucky, 1793-1794," *Filson Club History Quarterly,* XXII, 255–60; figures are from Boston *Columbian Centinel,* February 12, March 1, 1794.

defection of the French fleet. As a token of his commitment he forwarded $400, a sum quite inadequate for serious recruiting. Under normal conditions transit of mail was slow, but winter weather meant that Clark did not receive Genet's letter for several months, long after he had abandoned his plans.[23]

Washington had first learned of Genet's activities from the Spanish Commissioners in Philadelphia. In August, 1793, after the Commissioners reported that Genet was engaging agents familiar with Louisiana, Jefferson asked Governor Isaac Shelby of Kentucky to investigate. The Secretary of State warned the Governor that he must prevent American citizens from participating in an invasion of Louisiana, for this would be in violation of American neutrality. When Shelby replied in September, he indicated his willingness to cooperate with federal authorities although he had not observed any recruiting activity. In November, Jefferson again wrote Shelby, for the Spanish Commissioners now had the names of Genet's agents, one of whom was acting as an informer. Secretary of War Henry Knox also wrote Shelby and Arthur St. Clair, the Governor of the Northwest Territory, asking them to intervene forcibly if necessary.[24]

By the time these communications reached their destinations there was indisputable evidence that Clark was seeking recruits. St. Clair's response was prompt—on December 7, he issued a proclamation forbidding citizens from participating in any expedition directed at Spanish possessions. Governor Shelby's reaction, however, was quite different. Instead of following St. Clair's example, he preferred to assume an appearance of noncompliance as a means of pressuring the administration into taking stronger measures to advance Western interests. He felt secure in this course, for Clark was encountering insuperable obstacles. Few were willing to enlist under his command even with the allurement of a 1,000-acre land grant as a reward. Moreover, Clark's financial embarrassments were so great that

23. Lowitt, "Citizen Genet," *loc. cit.*, XXII, 260–65.

24. *Ibid.*, XXII, 263–64; Archibald Henderson, "Isaac Shelby and the Genet Mission," *Mississippi Valley Historical Review*, VI, 455–63; Keller, "Genet Mission," 450–59.

merchants declined to advance him credit for supplies or boats. Without ready money his prospects were hopeless. In replying to Jefferson on January 13, 1794, Shelby reported that Clark had a French commission, although as yet he had not raised any recruits and that two of Genet's agents were talking about organizing an expedition. Whether they would succeed or not, he felt unable to say, but he saw no reason to intervene unless he received "full and explicit" instructions from the President. Then, if the request lay within his constitutional power, he would execute the President's orders. Still, he doubted his authority to arrest members of an expedition before it reached its objective. Was it not legal for citizens to assemble, to carry arms, to travel in groups, and to leave the state? Could they be arrested simply because it was suspected that they were planning to invade Louisiana? Lest there by any doubt about his motives, he made his position clear: "I shall also," he wrote, "feel but little inclination to take an active part in punishing or restraining any of my fellow citizens for a supposed intention, only to gratify or remove the fears of the minister of a foreign prince who openly withholds from us an invaluable right and who secretly instigates against us a most savage and cruel enemy." [25] This plain language from a leading Westerner made disquieting reading in Philadelphia. Edmund Randolph replied in a strongly worded letter pointing out that Shelby had adequate authority under the militia act to check expeditions violating American neutrality. In an effort to appease Shelby, Randolph outlined in detail the current negotiations with Spain stressing the determination of the administration not to conclude an agreement which did not stipulate free navigation on the Mississippi.[26]

Shelby's letter to the Secretary of State accorded with local sentiment. After reading the Governor's letter, Senator James Brown of Kentucky, who had earlier advised his friends to have

25. Shelby to Jefferson, January 13, 1794, in Henderson, "Shelby," *loc. cit.,* VI, 461–62.

26. March 29, 1794, *ASPFR,* I, 155–56.

nothing to do with Genet's enterprise, agreed that it was "good policy" to display a "certain degree of unwillingness to oppose the project of an enterprise, which has for its object the free navigation of the Mississippi." He considered Shelby's letter timely, since he thought it possible that administration negotiations with Spain were being shrouded in secrecy to conceal arrangements unfavorable to the West.[27]

Although Fauchet had responded to administration protests by issuing a proclamation on March 6 which revoked Genet's commissions and admonished French citizens to observe American neutrality, it was felt that additional measures were needed to restrain Clark, even at the risk of offending Western sensibilities. There was considerable uncertainty, however, about the proper course to follow. The acquittal of Gideon Henfield (an American citizen tried for serving on one of Genet's privateers) had raised doubts about the validity and effectiveness of executive action as a means of enforcing neutrality. Consequently, the President turned to Congress for legislative implementation of administration regulations. The Senate acted promptly, but pro-French sympathizers in the House managed to postpone the bill. In view of what seemed to be threatening developments in the West, Washington resorted to a proclamation on March 24, warning citizens "to refrain from enlisting, enrolling or assembling themselves" in expeditions against nations with which the United States was at peace.[28]

Anxiety about Clark was not limited to Philadelphia. In New Orleans, the Governor of Louisiana, whose sources of information were as unreliable as those available to Washington, was so perturbed by reports that Clark had raised a force of 5,000 men that he requested reinforcements for his garrison. In view of the restlessness of the French residents, it was his belief that the colony could not be defended unless his forces

27. Brown to Shelby, February 16, 1794, in "Correspondence of George Rogers Clark and Edmond Genet," American Historical Association, *Annual Report for 1896,* I (Washington, D. C., 1897), 1040–41.

28. Freeman, *Washington,* VII, 155–56.

were augmented.[29] All these apprehensions were quite unjustified, for Clark lacked money—the most essential ingredient for launching an invasion. He managed to recruit a few men (probably not more than forty) and assembled a handful of flatboats at the mouth of the Ohio, but the expedition never departed. He was still seeking recruits when Fauchet's proclamation obliged him to suspend activities. There seems to be no foundation, other than vainglory or the hope of substantial payment, in his boast to Genet that he had a thousand men ready to attack Louisiana, when he was compelled to disband his forces.[30]

Although the administration was more worried about Clark's plans, the expedition against Florida reached a much more advanced state. Mangourit, the French Consul in Charleston to whom Genet had entrusted the invasion of Florida, was close enough to the scene of operations so that he did not have to rely on the uncertain communications which hampered Genet in arranging for a descent on Louisiana. Moreover, Mangourit was fortunate in that his agents enjoyed a much better standing than Clark, and hence were not so dependent upon the Consul's financial support. His most successful subordinate was Elijah Clarke, a revolutionary veteran and Indian fighter much admired in Georgia and South Carolina, who was commissioned a major general in the French army with a salary (it was never paid) of $10,000. Clarke's prestige and promises of land grants enabled him to recruit 300 men for an assault on St. Augustine. He mustered this force on the Georgia frontier in a position which suggested that he might be contemplating the expulsion of the Indians from territory assigned them in a federal treaty in 1790—a treaty universally condemned by the Georgians. In view of the readiness of Clarke's army, Mangourit wished to continue the operation after receiving Fau-

29. Keller, "Genet Mission," 460–62; James Alton James, *The Life of George Rogers Clark* (Chicago, 1929), 422–23.

30. Clark to Genet, April 24, 1794, Genet Papers, LC; James, *Clark,* 429–37.

chet's proclamation. The new Minister was sympathetic, but in the interest of restoring good relations with Washington, he ordered Mangourit to withdraw France's support. Even without French backing Clarke was able to keep a small band together until the fall of 1794, when the Governor of Georgia ordered it dispersed in response to administration wishes.[31]

Early in the summer of 1793 Jefferson had anticipated that the next session of Congress would not only give a decisive direction to American foreign policy but also place republican institutions on a secure footing. Yet, nothing that was done during the first session of the Third Congress came close to fulfilling these high expectations. There was no confrontation over foreign policy and the session ended with the two rival parties, which can now be appropriately called Federalist and Republican, almost evenly balanced. As in the past Washington's influence was decisive in swaying the views of Congressmen who classed themselves as independent or who were only peripherally committed to the Republicans. Unfortunately for the realization of Jefferson's wishes, public opinion did not exert the expected influence. Although the Federalists had not achieved a clear-cut victory during the summer, they had rallied support for the President's policy of neutrality and they had effectively embarrassed their opponents by publicizing Genet's threat to appeal to the people. To top this off the publication of Genet's correspondence scarcely provided the Republicans in Congress a suitable basis for attacking administration policy. Thus, even in the House, where the Republicans had a majority, a cautious approach was evident whenever the issues so bitterly debated in the past were raised. This is not to suggest that the session was free from strife for partisanship was more evident than ever before, but the Republican leaders wisely concentrated on issues offering greater chances of immediate success.

31. Keller, Genet Mission," 420–27, 577–83; E. M. Coulter, "Elijah Clarke's Foreign Intrigues and the 'Trans-Oconee Republic,' " *Proceedings of the Mississippi Valley Historical Society,* X, 260–74.

In the Senate, where the Federalists had such a narrow margin that they were frequently dependent upon the deciding vote of Vice President Adams, the main conflict centered about the determination of administration supporters to unseat Senator Albert Gallatin of Pennsylvania, who was closely identified with the Republican element. The Federalists devoted an inordinate amount of time—over a month—to this contest, before they succeeded in ousting him on the grounds that this Geneva born financier had not been a citizen of the United States long enough to meet the constitutional requirement for membership in the Senate.

In the House, then considered the more important branch of the legislature, the Republicans, expertly guided by Madison, sought to exploit public anger over the British Orders in Council by introducing resolutions advocating severe commercial reprisals against Great Britain. This proposal, in a variety of forms, kept the House in tumult for the greater part of the session, during which the Republicans, in order to strengthen their hand, organized public meetings to endorse Madison's resolves. In spite of public outrage over the Orders in Council (augmented by the conviction that the British were inciting the Indians), Madison's resolves were adopted in such a drastically modified form that the Republicans could not claim a significant victory. All that was done in a tangible way was the enactment of a thirty-day embargo. In the end the administration prevented Senate action on the resolves by sending John Jay to England to negotiate on current and past disputes. Washington whose choice of Jay was bitterly condemned by the Republicans, sought to appease the pro-French group and preserve his neutrality in the party conflict by naming James Monroe Minister to France. Thus as the session ended in June, 1794 administration policy remained much as it had been before—ostensibly neutral but with an undeniable English bias.

The controversies of the past were not entirely missing dur ing the session. The disagreement over the application c American neutrality still persisted, but, as far as one can judg from the incomplete record of debates in the *Annals of Congress,* it was expressed with few rhetorical flourishes. The President had suggested in his speech that Congress enact into law the administration rules concerning belligerents, which had proved difficult to enforce in the absence of specific statutes. Early in March, an administration sponsored bill was introduced in the Senate and promptly approved, though only with the deciding vote of the Vice President. In the House the critics of the administration said little but managed to delay action on the bill after the second reading. As the session drew to an end, Washington broke the deadlock by sending a special message to Congress on May 20. He reminded Congress that the activities of Clark made legislation urgent, and strengthened his plea by submitting the correspondence with Governor Shelby. When the House took up the bill on May 31, the Republicans shied away from directly assaulting the measure. Instead, Giles, Madison, and Wilson Cary Nicholas (also from Virginia) argued for postponement on the grounds that it was too late in the session to consider such an important measure. It is not surprising that they failed, in view of the President's direct plea in his message. The Republicans had to content themselves with the elimination (by a vote of 48 to 38) of the section barring the sale of prizes in the United States unless they had first been taken to a port of the sovereign of the captor. This was the only concession gained for France.[32]

The bill, enacted just a few days before the session ended, spelled out the neutrality regulations established during the preceding summer. It was not, of course, called a neutrality act, but bore the cumbersome title of "An Act for the punishment of certain crimes against the United States." The law confirmed Washington's policy, banning the outfitting of privateers, making it illegal to raise filibustering expeditions, and forbidding American citizens from enlisting in the military or naval service

32. *Annals of Congress,* 3C1S, 743–57, May 31–June 2, 1794; President's message and documents are in *ASPFR,* I, 154–60; Freeman, *Washington,* VII 155–57.

of foreign powers. The President was specifically empowered to use force to carry out the provisions of the act.[33]

Although Fauchet's initial contacts with the Washington administration went off well, he quickly discovered that in spite of the outward cordiality, he could obtain nothing more than his predecessor.[34] Within a matter of months after his arrival he found himself in the same position as Genet—negotiating with an ally who refused to grant advances on the debt, took no interest in an expanded commercial treaty, and manifested no the slightest intention of placing a more favorable interpretation on the Treaty of Commerce of 1778. Like Genet, he concluded that he was faced by an intractably aristocratic governmen firmly controlled by the pro-British element. He felt tha France's only hope, and this conviction was intensified after the ratification of Jay's Treaty, was to do everything possible bring the Republicans to power. This became the major theme of his dispatches, which, in their restrained language and sub stantial detail, were far more persuasive than Genet's had been Ultimately it was the determination to oust the Federalist which led the Directory to embark on a policy whose termina point was the quasi-war with France. American persistence i adhering to a policy of strict neutrality was incomprehensibl to the leaders of a nation committed to world revolution.

33. Thomas, *American Neutrality in 1793,* 278–79. The law prove defective in that it only prohibited acts of hostility against foreig powers by Americans within the territories of the United States. Th defect was remedied in 1797 when such offenses were also made illeg outside the borders of the United States. See Hyneman, *First America Neutrality,* 138.

34. DeConde, *Entangling Alliance,* 398–405.

12

Epilogue: Cornelia's Farm

LATE IN FEBRUARY, after settling the legation accounts with Fauchet (who reported confusion but no evidence of misappropriation), Genet slipped quietly from Philadelphia to the refuge of a friend's farm near Bristol. His departure from the capital, unnoticed by friends and enemies alike, marked his exit from public life. Just thirty-one, he had run his course at an age when most men were launching their careers. Though he lived another four decades, he never again held public office nor played a prominent role in politics. The former protégé of Marie Antoinette, royal civil servant, and one time Minister of the Republic of France passed the rest of his life as a gentleman farmer in New York State. Although he dared not return to France in 1794, he did not opt for a rural life entirely from necessity. Embittered by the injustice (as he saw it) meted out by Frenchmen who called themselves republicans and revolutionaries, his immediate mood was to flee public life. Like Candide, he wished only to live as a private citizen and find solace in cultivating his garden. As he told Cornelia, his sole desire was to settle in a country where virtue was honored and liberty respected; where a man who obeyed the law had nothing to fear from despots, aristocrats, or ambitious men.[1] In electing the life of a farmer, Genet was reenacting the romantic

1. Genet to Cornelia, February 24, 1794, Genet Papers, New-York Historical Society.

dream which had induced so many of his exiled compatriots to purchase farms in America hoping to find happiness living close to nature. In his case, the dream had all the more appeal, for his refuge would be shared by Cornelia, now that Governor Clinton had consented to their marriage.

After the wedding on November 6, 1794, at the Governor's official residence in New York, the newlyweds moved to a 325-acre farm near Jamaica, Long Island. Genet had purchased this property from DeWitt Clinton (the Governor's nephew and heir apparent to the family political domain) using Cornelia's dowry and money saved from his salary. Here, on "Cornelia's Farm" (as he named the property), their first child—a son and Genet's namesake—was born.[2] In 1802, Genet sold the Jamaica farm, moving his family to a larger estate, "Prospect Hill," overlooking the Hudson at Greenbush just three miles from Albany.[3]

The marriage seems to have been idyllically happy, never losing the romantic fervor of their courtship. Something of the depth of their attachment can be gathered from a letter Cornelia wrote her husband in 1801 during a prolonged separation: ". . . as to you, if I had a thousand hearts I would beg you to accept them, but as I have but one & that has been offered to you six years ago all I can do is to beg you to love it and cherish the girl who owned it before she gave it to you as much as she adores you." [4]

In 1794, Genet had wanted nothing more than life as a farmer, yet two years later he considered returning to France and resuming his career. The Jacobins were now gone, replaced by a moderate government—the Directory—which encouraged republican exiles to return and rewarded many with

2. Woodfin, "Genet," 541; George Clinton to Genet, October 25 1794, Genet Papers, New-York Historical Society; on the back of this letter is the note "Dot de Cornelia"; Receipt from DeWitt Clinton to Genet, June 16, 1794, Genet Papers, New York Public Library.

3. Genet to Cornelia, November 1802, Gratz Collection, Historical Society of Pennsylvania.

4. February 20, 1800, Genet Papers, LC.

government posts.[5] Some of Genet's associates (including Pascal, the Secretary of Legation) were safely ensconced in the Ministery of Foreign Affairs. Moreover, Genet's relatives had emerged from their enforced seclusion and occupied positions of importance. His brother-in-law, Auguié, was in the postal service and his sister, Mme. Campan, had opened a highly successful girls's school just outside Paris at Ste. Germaine-en-Laye. Through the parents and relations of her pupils (among them a daughter of Josephine Beauharnais and a sister of Napoleon), Mme. Campan had important official contacts. From both relatives and colleagues, Genet received a flow of letters urging him to return and assume the place to which his talents and patriotism entitled him.

Yet in spite of all these pleas Genet held back. His interest in returning home was not so much a matter of ambition, but stemmed from a determination to obtain a public vindication which would right the wrong done by his own country and reestablish his reputation in America, for he took it most unkindly that the national leaders of the Republican Party criticized him publicly. It is true that the son-in-law of George Clinton was honored by New York Republicans, but the Governor's influence could not guarantee him the same status elsewhere.

The most biting criticism of Genet was delivered by Republican Congressman William Branch Giles in the House of Representatives in May, 1797. Giles's speech was made in response to a message from President John Adams announcing the refusal of the French government to receive the newly appointed American Minister while tendering elaborate farewells to the departing James Monroe, recalled by President Washington. This action, according to Adams, was but another attempt to exploit what French officials erroneously believed to be a basic rift between the people of the United States

5. Woodfin, "Genet," 549; Greville Bathe, *Citizen Genet, Diplomat and Inventor* (Philadelphia, 1946), 24; Minnigerode, *Jefferson,* 369–73, 384–92; Didier, "Le citoyen Genet," *Revue des questions historiques,* XCIII (1913), 449; L. A. Pichon to Genet, August 2, 1796, Genet Papers, LC; Genet family letters in *Dawson's Historical Magazine,* XII (September, 1867), 155–59.

and the national administration. Republican orators challenged this interpretation, insisting that the Directory had refused to receive the new Minister because he had not been empowered to settle outstanding differences between the two nations. In elaborating on this theme, Giles noted that Genet had indeed attempted to create the impression that the people were hostile to administration policy, but no one had ever taken him seriously. The fact that the French Minister had been "universally reprobated" by all but a "few disorderly people" had been sufficient, according to Giles, to convince the French government that the Washington administration enjoyed the confidence of the nation. The trust of the people had further been proven by the many public resolutions in support of Washington's policy and condemning Genet. "Even the pulpit reviled Genet. If execration, disappointment, could fill up the measure of punishment, he [Genet] had it." [6]

This attack, delivered by a Republican once regarded as a friend, infuriated Genet, who was convinced that Jefferson was really behind the denunciation. His friends in New York were deeply sympathetic, feeling (as James Nicholson commented to his son-in-law, Albert Gallatin) that the Southern Republicans were behaving shabbily towards a man who had already suffered so much.[7] Genet vented his rage in a letter, ostensibly addressed to Jefferson but in fact intended for publication.[8] In this windy diatribe (which was neither sent nor published) he reviewed with considerable distortion the events of his mission and placed the blame for his downfall on the "deception" practiced by Jefferson. His case against the former Secretary of State rested on nothing more than the conviction, grown stronger with the years, that Jefferson had deliberately prevented him from utilizing popular sentiment, which he had mobilized in order to achieve the aims of his mission. This interpretation became an *idée fixe,* which he impressed on all who would listen. A hal

6. *Annals of Congress,* 5th Congress, 1st Session, 138–52, May 2[illegible] 1797.

7. July 2, 1797, Gallatin Papers, New-York Historical Society.

8. This letter dated July 4, 1797, is printed in Minnigerode, *Gene[illegible]* 413–25.

century after Genet's death, his son published a memoir asserting that Jefferson had played a double role, pretending to favor France while secretly working for an alliance with England.[9]

Since Genet was primarily concerned about a public vindication, he insisted on positive guarantees of preferment before returning to France. First, he asked that his name be removed from the list of émigrés and that his property be restored. This, perhaps, was not unreasonable, but his demand that he be given a diplomatic post—he even suggested reinstatement as Minister to the United States—was excessive. Although Mme. Campan exerted herself tirelessly in her brother's behalf, it was not until 1799, in the very last days of the Directory, that his name was struck from the list of émigrés and his property restored—if he returned within six months. This failed to satisfy the ex-Minister. Mme. Campan's influence increased after Napoleon seized power, but she still could not gratify her brother's demands. In 1804, when it was apparent that he would not be reinstated, Genet made the final break. At the age of forty-one he became a naturalized citizen of the United States.[10]

After his naturalization, Genet never returned to France. He kept in close touch with his relatives, but he felt too bitter over the ingratitude of his compatriots even to consider visiting his family. He had no reason to be dissatisfied with his decision to remain in America. His connection with one of the most important families in New York State gave him an assured social position, while his estate supplied him with a sufficient income to live in the leisurely style favored by the landowners scattered along the Hudson River.[11] His elegant manners, wit, charm, and musical talents assured him a gracious welcome at country parties and on his frequent visits to New York City. Genet spent much of his time in New York City, where he was drawn by the presence of Cornelia's family and by his varied business inter-

9. See George Clinton Genet, *Washington, Jefferson and "Citizen" Genet* (New York, 1899), 32–33.

10. See footnote 5 above.

11. Genet to Auguié, May 20, 1798, Genet Papers, New-York Historical Society.

ests. Like so many of his contemporaries Genet invested in the many new (and often highly speculative enterprises) of the day. On the whole his business ventures, which ranged from turnpike companies to manufacturing enterprises, were not successful. Two in particular—wool processing and plaster manufacturing—were disastrous. His business judgment was so defective that George Clinton limited Genet's control over the property left to Cornelia's children. The Governor's precautions were not entirely effective. Many years later Genet's eldest son quarreled bitterly with his father over the management of the family estate, and when Genet died in 1834 Prospect Hill was encumbered with mortgages contracted twenty years earlier.[12]

The family circle at Prospect Hill was broken for the first time when Cornelia died of consumption on March 23, 1810. Her death prostrated Genet, who (as he told his brother-in-law) was only saved from despair by the urgent need to care for his six children—the youngest but two years old.[13] Cheerful and optimistic in temperament, Genet gradually recovered and two years later was again enjoying the social diversions of Albany and New York. His "little talent for music," as he told his sister, made him an "indispensable associate" at ladies' parties all along the Hudson. Well aware of his standing as an eligible widower, he lightheartedly wrote his sister of the possibility of remarriage: "At first I reckoned 24 girls or young widows whom I admired and who seemed willing to regenerate my former happiness, but as I am not a Turk and could not marry them all I have by degrees reduced the number to three, to wit one in Albany, one in Poughkeepsie and one here, they are all three accomplished, captivating and wealthy. . . ."[14] His choice fell on Martha Brandon Osgood, daughter of Washington's Postmaster General, whom he married in 1814. This,

12. There are many items relating to these activities in the collections of Genet Papers. See George Clinton to Genet, August 6, 1809, and Petition of Martha Brandon Genet to the Legislature of New York, March 6, 1844 both in Genet Papers, New-York Historical Society.

13. May 5, 1810, Tallmadge Papers, New-York Historical Society.

14. Quoted in Woodfin, "Genet," 544.

like his first marriage, seems to have been a happy alliance.[15]

Until DeWitt Clinton's death in 1828, Genet busied himself with the family political interests. His activity was peripheral, for the notoriety attached to his name made it impossible for him to run for office or be given an appointment. He was valued as a propagandist, frequently writing newspaper essays and pamphlets under such pseudonyms as "Cassandra" or "An American Citizen." [16] His favored subjects were canal construction (which had the support of the Clinton interests), abolition of imprisonment for debt, and denunciation of the Southern domination of the Republican Party. Genet's most notable publications appeared in 1808 when New York Republicans ran George Clinton as a presidential candidate although he was at the same time vice presidential candidate on the national Republican ticket headed by James Madison. This stratagem was chosen by the New Yorkers as the most effective means of protesting the continued domination of the national party by Virginians and also of expressing their hostility to the Embargo. Genet's first entry in the contest was a cumbersomely entitled pamphlet—*Communication on the Next Election for President of the United States and on the Late Measures of the Federal Administration. With Notes, Illustrations and Documents. By a Citizen of New York.* Genet not only condemned the Embargo as a hopelessly ineffective measure since Britain was not dependent upon American shipping, but he went so far as to suggest that it had been framed to please Napoleon in the expectation that the Emperor would reward the United States with Florida. But what, asked Genet, could one expect from a government dominated by Virginians whose concern for Southern interests led to the neglect of the welfare of other sections. In a second pamphlet published later in the year he attacked Madison as secretly tainted with Federalism. In proof he submitted fragments from the notes kept by Robert Yates (a Clinton ally) during the Constitutional Convention of 1787.

15. Minnigerode, *Jefferson,* 400.
16. Many draft essays are in the various collections of his papers.

Genet strung these excerpts together to create the impression that Madison, as a member of the Convention, had wished to establish an all powerful central government by reducing the states to impotency.[17]

In his leisure hours at Prospect Hill, Genet renewed his youthful scientific pursuits, which he hoped would yield the fame (and perhaps fortune) that had eluded him as a diplomat. The results of his studies appeared in 1825 in a handsomely illustrated volume, *Memorial on the Upward Forces of Fluids.*[18] In this book he presented a number of inventions derived from what he described as a new scientific principle, namely, that fluids and gases were subject to a force of levity (the exact contrary of the force of gravity) which compelled them to move upwards. His most ambitious project was a method of pulling canal barges up inclined planes by harnessing the power generated when a hydrogen filled balloon rose freely in a silo-shaped building. Alternately he suggested that an air-filled copper tube in a deep well might be used in the same manner. He also revived an early project for providing balloons with a system of propulsion. His new suggestion involved equipping a cigar-shaped hydrogen balloon with a rudder and stabilizing wings, and using a horse-driven treadmill as a source of power for paddle wheels which would propel the balloon.[19]

These projects were more a tribute to his enthusiasm than to his scientific knowledge. As Thomas P. Jones, Professor of

17. The second pamphlet was entitled *A Letter to the Electors . . . of the United States* (Albany, 1808). This revelation of the secret proceedings of the Convention did not arouse much attention. In 1821, Genet published all of Yates's notes (the originals have since disappeared) in *Secret Proceedings of the Convention Assembled at Philadelphia. . . .* At that time he sent a copy to Monroe. Genet to Monroe, August 2, 1821, Genet Papers, LC.

18. This volume has a particular interest as the first book published in America dealing with aeronautics; it was reprinted in facsimile in 1969 by the Pemberton Press, New York.

19. For an excellent account of Genet's proposals see Bathe, *Genet, Inventor.*

Mechanics at the Franklin Institute, commented in a scathing review, Genet was so ignorant of mathematics and physics that he failed to realize that neither the balloon nor the copper tube were capable of generating the lifting force necessary to pull a barge. Moreover, Genet seemed unaware that machinery exerting a uniform force could not be used to pull barges of varying weights. Amidst these fanciful proposals, Genet included one practical suggestion, which went unnoticed. He recommended the use of air-filled tubes in ship construction as a means of preventing them from sinking. This arrangement, anticipating the use of airtight bulkheads, was utilized in the 1850s in the construction of unsinkable lifeboats. Disappointed by the hostile reception accorded his inventions, Genet consoled himself by attributing the criticism to envy, likening himself to Montgolfier and other practical inventors whose proposals had been greeted with derision only to be proven sound when given practical tests.[20]

Throughout his life Genet yearned for vindication. Since there was no hope of achieving this through public sources, he began, in his declining years, to write his memoirs. This personal testament, which merely reiterated the charges made in his unsent letter to Jefferson, was left unfinished when he died on July 14, 1834. The passage of four decades had dimmed public recollection of the troubling circumstances of his mission, and his death, like that of a private citizen, drew no special notice in the press. There was no public mourning, only the grief of his friends and relatives.[21]

20. Jones's review entitled "Baseless Fabric of a Vision," is in *American Journal of Science and Arts,* XIII (1828), 90–96; Genet's reply is in the same journal, XIII, 377.

21. Minnigerode, *Jefferson,* 403.

Bibliographical Note

THE MOST IMPORTANT SOURCES for Genet's mission are the official records of the two governments concerned. Most of these have been published. The correspondence between Jefferson and Genet will be found in *American State Papers, Foreign Relations,* Walter Lowrie and Matthew St. Clair Clarke, eds., I (Washington, D.C., 1832). This volume also contains letters to the American Minister in Paris. Genet's dispatches to the Minister of Foreign Affairs and his instructions are in Frederick Jackson Turner, ed., "Correspondence of the French Ministers to the United States, 1791–1797," *Annual Report of the American Historical Association for the Year 1903,* II (Washington, 1904). Since Turner did not include the dispatches from the Ministers of Foreign Affairs this basic collection must be supplemented by the archives of the Ministry of Foreign Affairs, the Archives des Affaires Étrangères, Correspondence Politique, États-Unis, of which photocopies are available in the Manuscript Division of the Library of Congress. In addition to these public sources Genet's private papers contain numerous drafts and copies of his official letters as well as many other items relevant to his mission. There are collections of his papers in the Library of Congress, the New-York Historical Society and the New York Public Library. Of these the collection in the Library of Congress is not only the most extensive but contains the largest quantity of official documents.

Next in importance are the writings of those involved directly with Genet. The letters and memoranda (known as the *Anas*) of Jefferson are most valuable for they provide essential detail about the conflict within the administration as well as the Secretary of State's private reactions. These are printed in Worthington C. Ford, ed., *Writings of Thomas Jefferson* (10 vols., New York, 1892–99).

Ford also reproduces a number of official notes not found elsewhere in print. Signficant material concerning administration policy will also be found in Harold C. Syrett, ed., *The Papers of Alexander Hamilton* (14 vols., New York, 1961–) and in John C. Fitzpatrick, ed., *The Writings of George Washington* (39 vols., Washington, 1931–44).

There are a number of secondary works indispensable for a study of the Genet Mission. Of these the most important is Alexander DeConde, *Entangling Alliance, Politics and Diplomacy under George Washington* (Durham, N.C., 1958). This was the first scholarly study of the foreign policy of the Washington administration and is particularly rich in its treatment of domestic political aspects and also of policy attitudes of European nations toward the United States. This work owes a large debt to Professor DeConde's book. Two biographies which provide invaluable supplemental material are Douglas Southall Freeman, John Alexander Carroll, and Mary Wells Ashworth, *George Washington* (7 vols., New York, 1948–57), and Dumas Malone, *Thomas Jefferson and His Time* (4 vols., New York, 1948–). Although subsequent works have added much to the understanding of the Genet Mission, Maude H. Woodfin, "Citizen Genet and His Mission" (unpublished Ph.D. dissertation, University of Chicago, 1928) is still useful. Particularly valuable for domestic political reaction to Genet and the Minister's ventures in the West is William Frederick Keller, "American Politics and the Genet Mission," 1793–1794 (unpublished Ph.D. dissertation, University of Pittsburgh, 1951). The whole question of neutrality has been explored in two basic works: Charles S. Hyneman, *The First American Neutrality: A Study of the American Understanding of Neutral Obligations during the Years 1792–1815* in *University of Illinois Studies in the Social Sciences,* XX (1934), Nos. 1–2, and Charles Marion Thomas, *American Neutrality in 1793. A Study in Cabinet Government* in *Columbia University Studies in History Economics and Public Law,* No. 350 (1931).

Although more books have been written about the Frenc Revolution than any comparable epoch in European history, ther is almost nothing in French historical works about French polic towards the United States or the Genet mission. Except for the ver brief period of Girondin dominance the United States did not figur very large in the thinking of France's political leaders. In discussin Girondin policy, I have had to rely (except for DeConde's previousl cited book) on general works dealing with the Girondins. Of thes the most important are A. Aulard, *The French Revolution: A Political History* (4 vols., London, 1910); Georges Lefebvre, *The French Revolution from its Origins to 1793* (2 vols., New York, 1962–64); M. J. Sydenham, *The Girondins* (London, 1961); and J. M. Thompson, *The French Revolution* (Oxford, 1964). Among the most useful works about the Girondin epoch is Eloise Ellery, *Brissot de Warville: A Study in the History of the French Revolution* (New York, 1915). French studies relating specifically to the Genet mission usually treat it from an American and not a French point of view. Only rarely do they use materials not accessible to American students. Among the more useful articles are L. Didier, "Le citoyen Genet," *Revue des questions historiques,* XCII (1912), 62–90, XCIII (1913), 5–25, 423–49, and Paul Mantoux, "Le Comité de salut publique et la mission de Genet aux États-Unis," *Revue d'histoire moderne et contemporaine,* XIII (1909), 5–35. Of little value are: Richard K. Murdoch, "The Genesis of the Genêt [*sic*] Schemes," *French American Review,* II (1949), 81–97, and Frederick A. Schminke, *Genet: The Origins of his Mission in America* (Toulouse, 1929). An indispensable guide to the shifting personnel in the French Ministry of Foreign Affairs is Frédéric Masson, *Le Département des affaires étrangères pendant la révolution, 1787–1804* (Paris, 1877).

The material relating to the early party conflict in the United States is voluminous. The works which have most influenced my point of view are: E. Noble Cunningham, *The Jeffersonian Republicans, 1789–1801* (University of North Carolina Press, 1957); Joseph Charles's penetrating essays in *The Origins of the American Party System* (New York, 1961); Irving Brant, *James Madison: Father of the Constitution, 1787–1800* (Indianapolis, 1957); and Dumas Malone's previously cited biography of Jefferson. The contemporary newspapers constitute an essential source along with the published writings of the leading political figures of the day.

American historians have long been interested in Genet's efforts to mount expeditions against Florida and Louisiana, even though these projects were notable failures. A considerable portion of the relevant documentation has been published: "Correspondence of George Rogers Clark and Edmond Genet," *Annual Report of the American Historical Association for the year 1896,* I (Washington, 1897), 930–1107; Frederick Jackson Turner, ed., "The Mangourit Correspondence in Respect to Genet's Projected Attack on the

Floridas, 1793–1794," *ibid.*, 1897 (Washington, 1898), 569–79; and Frederick Jackson Turner, ed., "Documents on the Relations of France to Louisiana, 1792–1795," *American Historical Review,* III (1897–98), 490–516. The best discussion of the background of these projects is in Frederick Jackson Turner's "The Origins of Genet's Projected Attack on Louisiana and the Floridas," *American Historical Review,* III (1897–98), 650–71. This masterly article has not been supplanted. Three scholarly articles summing up the evidence relating to various aspects of Genet's projects are: E. Merton Coulter, "Elijah Clarke's Foreign Intrigues and the 'Trans-Oconee Republic,'" *Proceedings of the Mississippi Valley Historical Society,* X (1918–1921), 260–79; Archibald Henderson, "Isaac Shelby and the Genet Mission," *Mississippi Valley Historical Review,* VI (1920), 445–69; and John Carl Parish, "The Intrigues of Doctor James O'Fallon," *ibid.*, XVII (1930), 230–63. Keller's previously cited unpublished dissertation has an extensive account of Genet's Western intrigues. Genet's activities had little impact on Canada. For this and subsequent French activities in Canada see Benjamin Sulte, "Les projets de 1793 et 1810," Royal Society of Canada, *Proceedings and Transactions,* Ser. 3, V (1911), 19–67.

The three collections of Genet papers noted in the first paragraph of this essay contain extensive biographical materials relating to all phases of his career and private life. When Genet came to America he brought with him family papers and many documents (copies and originals) from the files of the St. Petersburg legation. These are in the Library of Congress. There has been one full length biographical study of Genet, Meade Minnigerode, *Jefferson, Friend of France, 1793: The Career of Edmond Charles Genet . . . 1763–1834* (New York, 1928). Although based on a study of the relevant public and private documentary sources, the value of Minnigerode's work is vitiated by the author's pronounced anti-Jefferson bias and his excessively dramatic handling of the material. Most irritating is his habit of never dating an event or giving the date (either in the text or a note) of letters and other documents cited. While he covers Genet's mission in some detail, his prejudices render this section less valuable than his account of Genet's early career and his later years. Genet's son, George Clinton Genet published an account of the Genet Mission in 1899 under the title *Washington, Jefferson and "Citizen" Genet* (New York) which attempts to make Jefferson the villain of the piece. It contains material drawn from Genet's unpublished memoirs. Most useful for Genet's early life is Jules Jusserand, "La jeunesse de Citoyen Genet," *Revue d'histoire diplomatique,* XLIV (1930), 237–68. Jusserand prints extracts from family letters not found elsewhere. Also useful is Louis Franklin Genet, "Edmond Charles Genet," *Journal of American History,* VI (1912), 345–67, 489–504, 737–56.

Index